CROSSING THE RED LINE

From the Same Press

The Arrest of Hoveyda
Stories of the Iranian Revolution
Saïdeh Pakravan

The Folly of Speaking
The Seventh Tale
A Novel
Donné Raffat

At a Drop of a Veil
Marianne Alireza

CROSSING THE RED LINE

The Struggle for
Human Rights in Iran

Mehrangiz Kar

With a preface by
Majid Tehranian

Toda Institute for Global Peace and
Policy Research

Blind Owl Press
An imprint of
Mazda Publishers, Inc. 2007

Blind Owl Press
An Imprint of
Mazda Publishers, Inc.
P.O. Box 2603
Costa Mesa, California 92628 U.S.A.
www.mazdapub.com

Library of Congress Cataloging-in-Publication Data
Kar, Mehrangiz.
Crossing the red line: the struggle for human rghts in Iran/
Mehrangiz Kar.
p.cm.

ISBN: 1-56859-192-6 (alk. paper)

1. Kar, Mehrangiz. 2. Women—Iran—Biography. 3. Feminists—
Iran—Biography. 4. Women's rights—Iran. 5. Human rights—
Iran. I. Title.
HQ1735.2.Z75K36 2006
305.420955—dc22
[B]
2006046197

Dedicated to my daughters, Lily and Azadeh, for whom tranquil childhood were often compromised due to my social and professional endeavors

Preface

This is a remarkable book. It chronicles the life of a woman in Iran under the monarchical and Islamic regimes. Under both regimes, she was a leading feminist activist and human rights lawyer. From such unique perspective, Mehrangiz Kar ties together micro and macro histories to provide a feminist, intellectual, and political portrait of Iran during the 1960s and after. The volume deserves to be read by both generalists and specialists on Islamic law and revolutionary change in Iran. Mehrangiz Kar and Shirin Ebadi, the Nobel Laureate for Peace in 2004, have become symbols of the counter-intuitive effects of history. The Islamic Revolution of 1979 in Iran was initially a delayed constitutional revolution. It had been long postponed by foreign interventions to prevent the fruition of the Constitutional Revolution of 1905-09. Largely due again to another foreign intervention in the form of Iran-Iraq War of 1980-88, the revolution turned into an extremist venture. It devoured its own children and civil liberties. It did so in the name of Shi'a Islam, a medieval worldview and legal system that determined life in minutest detail. As a consequence, the position of women suffered a great deal. *hejab* (veiling), polygamy, and diminution of human rights at half the rights of men, were restored. Women responded with vigor and veracity. As a result, today Iran can claim a higher percentage of women university enrolment than men. Women can be found in executive, legal, medical, and university positions. Iranian women in diaspora, such as Sattareh Farman Farmaian and Azar Naficy, have won accolades for their books. Shirin Ebadi and Mehrangiz Kar are admired throughout the world for their human rights efforts in Iran. The struggle for human and women rights is not, however, finished in Iran—and elsewhere.

This book occupiers a special place in the study of Iran and human rights. It is engaging because it tells the story from the perspective of a lawyer involved in the details of her work. It provides a deep insight into the historical processes of social change, demonstrating the current problems of an uneven world. Globalization has brought tribal, agrarian, commercial, industrial, and digital societies into intimate, face-to-face contact. The economic, political, and cultural trappings of each of these enormously different societies belong to diverse layers of history. As we are witnessing in Afghanistan and Iraq, their encounter and imposition of one set of values upon another produces quixotic and often violent consequences. The onset of World Ware III in the form of global terrorism may be one of the consequences of the glaring global disparity in economic, political, and cultural conditions.

What is to be done in the face of such yawning chasms? Different strategies present themselves: First, ignore the gaps— ignore it and the problem will go away. However, the problem does not and cannot go away. Second, help out in disasters. The Asian Tsunami of 2004 provided an opportunity for the more affluent to help out the less affluent. Third, forcefully intervene to reconstruct traditional societies along more modern institutions. As in Vietnam and Iraq, however, the road to hell is paved with good intentions. Fourth, take a multilateral approach and through the machineries of global governance (e. g. UN and its specialized agencies) redress some of the worst conditions. This is a laudable and incremental path fraught with multilateral headaches. Fifth, struggle for a new world order— more just, less violent, and with luck, a bit more harmonious and peaceful.

These strategies are not mutually exclusive. Iran presents a case study of how an oil dependent economy can be sensitive to international pressures for human rights. Iranian society needs to catch up. That spells out equality for women. The rest of the world can ignore, impede, or help out in this process. Mehranguiz Kar's book shows how. The Toda Institute is proud to have sponsored this volume by offering her a Senior Peace Fellowship.

The Persian version of this volume will appear soon. It will update the material and reach out to the Persian speaking community throughout the world. However, the views expressed in this book clearly belong to the author and do not necessarily represent the Toda Institute.

Majid Tehranian,

Director, Toda Institute for Global Peace & Policy Research
Adjunct Professor of International Relations,
Soka University of America
June 24, 2006

1

I arrived in this world about 61 years ago, in 1944, in the *south-ern* city of Ahvaz, in Iran. In the tradition of all Muslim families, a believing member of the household took me, the bundled up newborn, from the hands of Mama Jamileh, the midwife who had delivered me, and recited the *azan*, or the call to prayer, in my ear.

Allahu Akbar
Allahu Akbar
Allahu Akbar
Allahu Akbar

Ash-hadu an la ilaha ill-Allah
Ash-hadu an la ilaha ill-Allah

Ash-hadu anna Muhammad-an-Rassoolullah
Ash-hadu anna Muhammad-an-Rassoolullah

Asha-hadu anna Ali-an-Vali-Allah
Asha-hadu anna Ali-an-Vali-Allah

Hayya 'alas-Salah
Hayya 'alas-Salah

Hayya 'alal-falah
Hayya 'alal-falah

Allahu Akbar
Allahu Akbar

God is most great

God is most great
God is most great
God is most great

I bear witness that there is none worthy of being worshipped except for God Allah
I bear witness that there is none worthy of being worshipped except for God Allah

I bear witness that Muhammad is the Apostle of (God) Allah
I bear witness that Muhammad is the Apostle of (God) Allah

I bear witness that Ali is the representative of (God) Allah [1]
I bear witness that Ali is the representative of (God) Allah

Come to prayer
Come to prayer

Come to success
Come to success

God is most great
God is most great

In honor of one of the most revered women, who was the Pharaoh's wife and who educated Moses, the voice called me Assieh and blew in my ear. My eyes were closed, but my ears could hear. I can imagine the warmth of my grandmother's breath while she recited the *azan* in my ear. For the first time, she entered the sound of Arabic words into my infant memory. If my father had not been a Muslim, Bibi, my grandmother, would not have been allowed to recite the *azan* for me. From the instant I was born into the human race, I followed in the footsteps of my father and became a Shiite. And despite the fact that I had not willed it, and had no say in the matter, with my birth, there was one additional Muslim in the world.

---

[1] Recited only by Shiite Muslims, who acknowledge Ali, son-in-law of the Prophet, as the rightful successor to Muhammad in leading Muslims and the Muslim world.

It took a few days before I could acquire Iranian nationality. The only person who could pass on Iranian nationality to me was my father. One day, my father came home with a box of sweets and a birth certificate. By that time my eyelids were open and I could see him, a Muslim, an Iranian and a man. Even in that stage of infancy, I came to realize his power, and knew that whatever I had was because of him. Upon my birth, he bestowed upon me his religion and his beliefs, and now I could see that he had given me his nationality as well. He gave the birth certificate to my mother for safekeeping, and she read from it in a loud voice, "Mehrangiz, the child of Mostafa and Batoul."

I watched their strange behavior, while sucking on my pacifier. I placed my name in an appropriate place within my senses and my memory. I could not speak, but I could hear and see. I can imagine the smell of incense that was burned in my honor on that day, and can picture the small tin can in which it burned. I imagine the strange movements of the hand that circled the can around my head and the sounds of prayers intended to keep me safe from evil. On that day, my grandfather gave me a small silver-encased Koran to hang around my neck. The necklace was heavy and rubbed against my bare skin. I bellowed, in an effort to demonstrate my discomfort. But my fits were in vain. Slowly, I became accustomed to it, although still, my skin and bones and flesh were irritated by the mere presence of this charm, especially as I rolled around in my crib. In protection, I was forced to control all my movements, even as I slept. One day as my mother undressed me for a bath, she noticed that the little charm, which held in it a yellow paper Koran, had scratched my skin. My mother removed my grandfather's present from around my neck. She said a little prayer and touched the Koran to her lips, and then placed it on the shelf. She would not allow the members of our household to steal my comfort, even if it were with the intent of safeguarding tradition and sacred rituals.

Slowly, I realized that I shared my "gender" with my mother. It was her inherent right to transfer her feminine characteristics to her child. My mother flaunted her femininity as if she were proud of it. I never understood why. The other women in my life were not like my mother. They acted as if they were lacking. I despised them and was happy that I too was lacking—lacking the male gender that was! Now that I think about the past, I realize I became a feminist at the precise moment when I grew to understand that I shared with my mother her gender and that my body was like hers.

For a long while, I paid no attention to what my father had bestowed upon me—my religion and my nationality. At noon, the radio would broadcast the sound of the *azan*, to call the Muslims for noon prayers. The members of my household would gather together for lunch, which we ate on the floor. The sound of the *azan* was the continuation of Bibi's voice, which echoed in my ear. On occasion, my brothers, Houshang and Fereydoun, would bring home colored paper. With this paper they would build flags and I came to understand that the colors green, white and red represented our nationality.

While I was still tackling the elementary concepts of life, the Second World War came to a close. The people of the world had made a pact to create and maintain a new world order, and to seek refuge in the protection it offered. The peaceful nature of humanity wanted to overtake and tame its violent nature. They were drafting the Declaration of Human Rights, which guaranteed individuals the right to choose freely their religion and their nationality. I could not be a witness to all that was happening. My world was small and confined. I did not believe that what I had inherited naturally from my parents would haunt me in the years ahead, and that I would be forced to take part in conflicts related to issues of gender, religion and nationality for a lifetime to come.

But of course, I do realize that my gender was mine, and my sex a result of nature. I can imagine today Mama Jamileh, the midwife, handling my naked infant body in her blood-drenched hands and upon my birth announcing to all those present, "It's a girl; God willing she will be honorable." Years passed before I realized what it meant for a girl to be honorable. It meant to maintain virginity, to remain chaste, until the night of marriage, when the groom was allowed to protrude beyond the hymen, or the curtain of chastity, and a young girl could—with a few drops of blood on the white of her sheets, which would later be passed around for viewing by family members—prove that she was indeed honorable.

*****

I was growing up in a house that had a yard and a fountain in the courtyard and many rooms. The room with five doors was the gathering place for the members of our family. My mother would rent the other rooms and with the income would manage the household and the family. Very quickly, I came to realize that my father, besides what he had bestowed upon me at the time of my birth—my religion and nationality—was not able to give me much else. He was an illiterate man, eternally in awe of my mother, who could read not only the Koran, but also poems by Hafez and the *Shahnameh* (Book of Kings). My mother was busy with her own work and would become restless with the presence of my father.

She often recounted the story of how they came to wed: "He asked for my hand in marriage with a gun in tow. He threatened Bibi. He told her that he would kill us all if she refused to allow me to marry him. He married me by force."

My mother was 9 when she was forced to marry my father. She would run away from him, from his touch, the feel of his unshaven face, and take refuge on the rooftop, where he could not touch her. To this story, she would always add that in the end, my father had promised not to touch her. Since the day of the promise, my father would place his gun between himself and my mother in bed, allowing her in advance the right to take his life should he happen to break his promise.

With this agreement, my 9-year-old mother hugged her little doll at night, and rested peacefully. And that violent, illiterate and love-stricken man stayed true to her and waited until she reached the age of 13 and agreed to become a woman.

In the house in which I grew up, two women were in charge: my mother and my grandmother, Bibi. My father was not a civilized man. He only understood one thing: that he was in love with Batoul, a fact he often declared out loud. When he wanted to compliment my mother, he would say that she was not a woman, but rather that she was an angel. Bewildered by the fact that my mother would still run away from him, as she did in her childhood, and would not let anyone forget that her husband had married her by the force of a gun, my father admired her. All other women he viewed disparagingly. My mother would take revenge upon my father at every opportunity and would work to make up for that which she had lost at his hands. She had managed to learn how to read and write from neighbors, and in her youth she had come to love the poet Hafez. Bibi could only read the Koran and believed steadfastly that people needed to be educated only to the point which allowed them to read the word of God. Literacy, in her mind, was of no other use.

I was 5 years old when a new development took hold of our home. My oldest brother, Fereydoun, who was 16 years my senior, had embarked upon a life of poetry and literature, and as a result had managed to bring to the city of Ahvaz, and to our home, the literary community. With the entrance of this intellectual factor, the contradictions and conflicts escalated. By force, Fereydoun had managed to take control of one of the rooms in our house, and had made it off limits to the other members of the household. And as such, I became the quiet witness to Bibi's incantation of the Koran, my mother's recitation of the poetry of Hafez, the drunken fits of my father, and Fereydoun's intellectualism.

There existed a quiet struggle between Bibi and my mother. This mother and daughter, without ever allowing their conflict vivid expression, were at constant war. It took me many years and the experience of the revolution before I understood that the challenges facing my mother and Bibi were in fact a manifestation of the struggle between tradition and modernity.

Bibi's *hejab*, or Islamic dress, was an A'ba, or covering that could be traced in its roots to Arab cultures. This was different than the Iranian version of the Islamic dress, which was usually a *chador*. The A'ba was a particular form of covering unique to Arab women. In Khuzestan province, where we lived, both Arab women and local Khuzestani women of my mother's and grandmother's generations would usually wear the A'ba. Confronted with the thinking of her daughter and her grandson, Bibi felt alone. Bibi's husband, Baba Taghi, who was my mother's stepfather, and who always treated us as if we were his own grandchildren, was not supportive of her. Of course, he was a believer. He even participated in religious mourning festivities in honor of the Prophet's grandson Hossein, and headed the procession of men who pounded their chests in a demonstration of grief for Hossein's martyrdom. But, he was also a steadfast admirer of

Ms. Pouran, the most popular vocalist of the time, and—paying no mind to Bibi's objections – he would blast the sound of her voice from the radio in our home. He was also addicted to opium, and at night he would listen to music as he smoked his opium. He would teach me how to clean his opium pipes so that he could later smoke the residue. Baba Taghi had a coffee shop on 30-Meter Street in Ahvaz. Sometimes he would take me to the coffee shop with him, where I could watch the men drink tea, smoke their tobacco with hookah pipes and sing while they discussed the politics of the British.

Bibi slowly reached the conclusion that she needed to propagate her ideas, even if in secret. The minute I turned 9, Bibi used every opportunity, especially in the absence of my mother, to pull me aside to recite religious narration and teachings. She would ask me to put on a *chador* (Islamic dress) and to pray alongside her. She even sewed me a *chador*, and when for the first time I put it on, an uncontrollable happiness overtook her. She kept saying, "You can't imagine how beautiful you look with the *chador*." Bibi taught me how to pray. I would stand next to her in prayer and would mimic her motions. Up to this point, my mother had no objections. But the minute she learned that Bibi was trying to convince me to wear a *chador* to school, she threw a fit and warned her mother to let me be.

These two women had one common characteristic: They both demonstrated innate leadership qualities. Each used the facilities available to her to attract followers. Bibi's weapons of choice were the Koran and religious narrations and teachings. Reciting Hafez's poetry and discussing issues related to health were the strategies employed by my mother. She had taken to reading health brochures that she found in doctors' offices and health magazines, and felt compelled to share her newfound knowledge with the women in our community.

People in our city who wanted to try something new or needed to make decisions on important matters would go to Bibi, who, upon consulting the Koran, would advise them on which path to choose. If someone had a dream and needed an interpretation, he would go straight to Bibi. My grandmother was a skillful talker, and having listened to so many sermons, she was well positioned to take the pulpit as she often did—albeit her pulpit was confined to her own room. This is how she proliferated her beliefs. She always had a pot of tea brewing on the samovar, and a hookah lit for visitors. She would wrap her A'ba around her body and direct the minds of her visitors toward that which she felt was right. Her speech was eloquent and determined. Both men and women listened to her and followed her advice. She explained the decree of God as she understood it, and she had become so well versed in interpreting dreams that at times I felt astonished. She used all the religious symbolism at her disposal to interpret the dreams of those who consulted her.

Many years later, upon reading the works of Jung, I longed for Bibi. Having moved from Shiraz to the backward city of Ahvaz in Khuzestan, in search of a new breadwinner to replace her dead husband, my grandmother, Bibi, was well versed in the language of symbolism. Although confined to her own thinking and within the limits of her own experience, she could fully compete with Jung.

My mother had become the talk of the town. Her ability to re-cite the poetry of Hafez was unparalleled. She utilized every op-portunity to read the poetry of Hafez and had become so well versed in interpreting his poetry that people were naturally drawn to her. All who wanted their fortunes told using one of Hafez' poems would come to our house. My mother, in ritualis-tic fashion, would never touch a book of Hafez without Wudhu (ablution), and as if in a religious trance, she would recite the following words:

Oh Hafez of Shiraz
The guardian of all secrets
I swear you to Ali the Saint
And to your lover Shakhe Nabat
Reveal to this believer his future

Sometimes the believer was a man, and sometimes a woman. Although her gatherings were mixed, when at home, my mother was not accustomed to wearing the *chador*. She was respected equally by both men and women, but my mother was at her best at all-women gatherings. These celebrations, organized and managed by my mother, at times included the recitation of the religious verse (*mowludi*) in honor of the birth of the 12th Imam, the Shiite messiah. At other times, the celebrations were dedicated to reading the poetry of Hafez, and on occasion they included music and dance. Bibi only participated in the religious celebrations, as only those were legitimate in her eyes.

My mother and grandmother, without even realizing it, each represented certain characteristics of Iranian society—a society that I only realized many years later is one filled with contradictions and complex intricacies. My mother worked to reconcile the Islamic traditions with the Iranian ones, all the while trying to maintain balance. Music, poetry and health education, were the tools of her trade. To make her gatherings festive, she invited female musicians to play the tar[2] and the tambourine. At every opportunity, she would retell, for all the women in the neighborhood, what she had learned in her health magazines. Passing on her knowledge of health was a passion. In our house, my mother was the spokesperson for Western culture and thought. Her insistence on the celebration of Noruz, the Iranian New Year, according to its Zoroastrian heritage, was unsettling to Bibi. Through an unspoken and unacknowledged agreement, my mother and Bibi tolerated one another.

From my earliest memories, I recall that my mother would honor the death of Hossein, the grandson of the prophet Mohammad, during the 10 days of mourning before the day of *Ashura* during which Hossein and his followers were slain. During these 10 days, all the women of the neighborhood would volunteer to help her. They would help break sugar cubes, bring cups and saucers for the event and sprinkle rose water, to make the house smell nice. Finally, there would inevitably be a woman whose prayers to God for a male child during past mourning festivities had been answered. True to tradition, she would place her infant in Ali Asghar's crib, a small green crib representing the crib of Hossein's youngest child, also killed along with his father on the day of *Ashura*. Men also commemorated the death of Hossein by traveling in mourning groups around town. They would carry the crib around from neighborhood to neighborhood, allowing women to uphold their vow to God by placing their male child in the crib.

This was the house in which I grew up. While the Islamic and Iranian identities that existed in this house created challenges,

---

[2] Iranian stringed musical instrument

the conflict was never a violent one. All of the members of the household enjoyed taking part in social gatherings. It was a known fact in town that the home of Batoul was open to both believers and nonbelievers. Surprisingly, not only did people not have a problem with my mother, they admired her. When they wanted to praise her, they would do so by stating that she was not a woman and that they wished that wives were more like Batoul.

This peaceful life was suddenly disturbed by Fereydoun's intellectualism. All of a sudden, new thoughts, ideas and words entered our home. With his entrance to the intellectual community, the comings and goings in our town and house changed as well. One day, Nezam Vafa[3], a well-known poet, came to Ahvaz at the invitation of Fereydoun. Another day, the poetess Forough Farrokhzad[4], who at the time was living with her husband in Ahvaz, visited our house. Fereydoun's books of poetry and literature were a surprising addition to the book of Kings, the collection of Hafez's poems, the Koran, and the health magazines that already existed in our home. For the first time in my memory, there was an unfamiliar addition to the furniture in our house. My mother bought a cupboard with shelves, which they called a bookcase, to store the growing collection of Fereydoun's books.

*****

On the outskirts of the city in which I was born, in accordance with traditional tribal customs, girls were beheaded. Honor killings were regular and exciting news in our town. Dawns were

---

[3] Nezam Vafa (1883-1960) was a lyric poet who wrote love poems in the classical style, as well as pieces of romantic poetical prose.

[4] Forough Farrokhzad was born into a middle-class family in Tehran on January 5, 1935. One of seven children, Forough attended public schools and in 1951, at the age of 16, married Parviz Shapour. The two were separated in 1954. Forough published five collections of poetry. Her poetry describes her feelings about conventional marriage, the plight of women in Iran, motherhood, and women's sexuality. Forough's vivid expressions of love and sexuality and the concept of enjoyment of sexuality in her poems were revolutionary and mark the first such expression among women poets in Iran. Forough died in 1967 at the age of 32 and at the height of her creativity.

painted red with the blood of young innocent native girls, and the news of their murders would travel by word of mouth as a warning to all children born female who were expected at the age of 9 to conduct themselves as pious Muslim adult women, safeguarding themselves from the eyes of men to whom they were not related. On occasion, the murderous members of the household, who in defense of their family's honor had beheaded a young woman accused of sexual relations with a man, would place the girl's head outside the front door of their home, so that with the breaking of dawn, the community could bear witness to their honor, their pride and their prejudice. Later I found that some interpretations of Islam, and even some of the laws during the time of Mohammad Reza Pahlavi, the Shah of Iran, supported and provided legal justification for the actions of these murderers. Article 179 of the general penal code during the time of the Shah did not prosecute men who had killed their wives due to suspicion of adultery, and limited the penalty for such acts in the case of fathers and brothers of the woman. Specifically, this article stated that should a man witness his wife engaged in a sexual act or in a situation resembling or indicative of sexual relations with a strange man, and in response he murders, injures or assaults either or both of them, he would not be subject to penalty under the law. Should a man witness his daughter or sister engaged in a sexual act or an in a situation resembling or indicative of sexual relations with a strange man, and commits murder in response, he would be subject to imprisonment for a term of one to six months, and in the case of assault or injury, he would be subject to a term of 11 days to two months imprisonment.

The neighborhood in which we lived was not too far from the outskirts of town, where the native Arab tribal populations lived. So, the image of young girls drenched in their own blood was a common image that often haunted me during my younger years, both in reality and in my imagination and dreams. I spent my childhood years in this feverish atmosphere, where the killing of women was an old tradition. In these frightful surroundings where they killed women in love, Fereydoun, upon entering young adulthood, began writing love poems, and through this medium he defended and promoted the rights of lovers. Tenderness had become the spice that adorned the primitive life of the

Arab tribes, and this was a source of joy and excitement. My brother would build poems and I would stare at his lips as he recited them. Every day, he would bring with him to our home an incident that was an example of resistance to injustice, ignorance and superstition. With his poetry and song, Fereydoun would incite the anger of those who, in the years 1939-1959 in that far away city, would murder women for the sake of defending honor. He was a simple person and believed that he could combat ignorance and superstition, which stood in the path of freedom and justice, with poetry and song.

I remember the day I turned 5 and they wanted to pierce my ears. One of the women from our community used a heated sewing needle with thread running through it to do so. The thread was then tied into a loop to ensure that the holes would stay open. Despite the fact that I was crying from pain and fear, I felt a special excitement in the pit of my stomach. A pair of ruby earrings would soon adorn my ears. The members of our house shared my excitement and each viewed this moment as a special occasion that attested to my maturation—an occasion that in a few short years would be followed by my official entrance into womanhood. On that day, my mother burned incense in my honor and my grandmother sewed me a cloth doll.

At noon when Fereydoun came home, the situation changed quickly. He was infuriated at the site of my tearful eyes and bloody ear lobes. He cursed the members of our home and began to cry uncontrollably. "You are teaching my sister the customs of slavery. You are bringing her up as if she were indentured, with hoops in her ears," he declared.

My mother and Bibi quietly laughed at Fereydoun and I could not understand what he was saying. A few days passed and the wounds on my ears began to heal. Fereydoun also calmed down. But before the ruby earrings could replace the sewing thread that looped from my ear lobes, Fereydoun took me to see a film. In our town there was only one cinema house and it showed only Arab and Indian films. Going to the cinema was a dream come true for girls my age. After the film, Fereydoun took me to a pharmacy, and with a soft piece of cotton dowsed in alcohol he removed the dirty, blood-covered loops of thread that hung from my ears. Then we went to a pastry shop and sat at a table for two, across from one another. He spoke to me as if I were an adult. He told me stories about slavery and in the end he made me promise to forget about the ruby earrings forever. The sweet taste of the cream-filled pastry distracted me and I did not hear all that he had said, but that night, I had a dark image of the concept of slavery and the earlobes of the female slaves, adorned with hoops an image that has stayed with me forever.

That afternoon, after he had made me promise to forget the earrings and in the fashion of adults we had shook hands to seal our pact, Fereydoun took me to a photography studio, which was the only modern studio of its kind in our city. There, he removed the photographer's tie and used it to pull back my long braided hair, like a Westerner's. I could see that Fereydoun was pleased. He picked me up and placed me on a chair, and as he stood next to me, he asked the photographer to take a picture of us. When the picture was ready, Fereydoun blew it up and framed it, placing it on the shelf in the room with five doors.

"This is how a little girl should look. Her hair is short and it does not bother her, and she does not have hoops hanging from her ears. She is free," he declared.

*****

The intellectual onslaught of Fereydoun changed the careful balance of our home and created instability. Slowly, the presence of my mother and Bibi was overshadowed by Fereydoun, who had filled the space of our home. Serving Fereydoun's friends and visitors didn't leave much time or energy for the women of the home to continue enjoying life according to their own traditions and likings.

After he turned 18, Fereydoun was no longer an individual. Instead he became a symbol of the new intellectualism that was overtaking the city of Ahvaz. The center and focus of this intellectualism was decorated with the poetry of Nima Yushij[5], the

---

[5] Nima Yushij (whose real name was Ali Esfandiari) was born in November 1897, and grew up in Yush, in Mazandaran Province. Yushij is known as the pioneer of modern Iranian poetry. His poem "Myth," published in 1922, is largely known as the poem that set the foundation for the development of modern poetry in Iran. In modern Iranian poetry, rhythm takes center stage, and poets compose their according to

pioneer of modern Iranian poetry. Yushij had broken with the tradition that for hundreds of years had dictated the format of poetry, and had sparked a major development in the literary community in Iran. Fereydoun was a charismatic and handsome man. My other brother Houshang, who was eight years my senior, could not tolerate the attention that Fereydoun received at home and in intellectual circles, and at times, in an effort to receive attention of his own, he would do strange things.

One day, the world of my childhood was turned upside down. They informed my mother that Fereydoun had been beaten up in high school. In hysterics, my mother took Fereydoun to the clinic, and over night, she made arrangements for him to attend school in Abadan, a town 100 kilometers from Ahvaz. Fereydoun left Ahvaz with bandages around his head. They claimed that he had become a nonbeliever, that he had been blasphemous, and that he had promoted, among the youth of the city, the thinking of Ahmad Kasravi. I heard that a group of merchants with children in school had decided, because of his adherence to Kasravi, to force Fereydoun to leave town. First, they had arranged to have him beaten. They had then let my mother know that if her son decided to stay in Ahvaz he would be killed. Fereydoun left and his absence could be felt throughout our home. My mother would go to the telephone house in Ahvaz on a daily basis to contact her son. She could not hide her worry and to calm her nerves she began to put a cigarette between her lips. Slowly the smoke of cigarettes became an added feature of our home.

As a child I could not understand the meaning of blasphemy and disbelief, nor could I understand why they would want to kill someone who had come to doubt his religion. It took years before I understood that Kasravi was a cleric who had objected to those who, while professing belief in Islam, were in reality hypocrites and had promoted superstition in the name of religion. Kasravi called those clerics, who—cloaked under the protection offered by religion and their robes—prevented people from intellectual growth, traitors to both Iran and Islam. He believed that by outing these people, he would be able to save a society

---

the rhythm of natural speech, rather than a set of predetermined meters or "vazn." Yushij died in 1959.

that was addicted to superstition and hypocrisy. In the beginning, they would attack Kasravi's followers, and then in 1946 they killed Kasravi with a bullet, calling themselves the Martyrs of Islam[6]. With his death, these worries, too, were put to rest.

This was the first time that I remember violence being committed in the name of religion. Before this, I associated religion with the sound of the noon *azan* calling believers to prayer, the sound of Bibi's voice reading from the Koran, the *Ashura* mourning festivities, religious sermons, the smell of rose water, the sweet taste of rice pudding, the mourning of death, the breaking of fast in Ramadan, and celebrations in honor of the birth of the prophet and his decedents. For me, and for all the children of Ahvaz, religious ceremonies were an opportunity for us to come together and play. The passion plays of *Ashura* in honor of the heroic battle of Hossein nearly 1,400 years ago, which would take place in our streets and community, opened a new world of theater to us. As a child, the best times of the year for me were the religious months of Ramadan, Moharram and Safar, and the Noruz holiday celebrations.

In my childhood dreams, native Arab girls whose heads had been severed due to sexual relations with their lovers would come alive. There were certain other events that would complete the cycle of religious violence in my ruffled mind. One day I saw that they had piled up Fereydoun's books in the courtyard of our house and set them aflame, so that, upon hearing the news, those believers who had promised violence would finally let us be. On another day I was witness to the only time when my father and Bibi conspired to set to fire Houshang's tar, the stringed instrument my mother had bought for him. Through the grapevine, my father had heard that my bother Houshang was becoming a common musician and in that tradition had taken to swinging his head back and forth when he played the tar. I was astonished at

---

[6] Ahmad Kasravi Tabrizi (1890-1946) was born in the city of Tabriz. As a young man he entered a seminary in Tabriz to become a Shiite cleric and became a mullah at the age of 20. Armed with his knowledge of religion and Islam he began to question the behavior of the clergy, including hypocrisy, greed, abuse of religion and religious power, their disinterest in contemporary problems of society, and their divisive influence, especially their opposition to the constitutional movement, which Kasravi supported.

their distaste and dislike for musicians. All of the children and women I knew loved musicians, and when we went to weddings, we were able to see and experience first hand the joy and hope their music created in listeners. Houshang, at the behest of my mother, was taking music classes offered by a local musician. Of course, later on, I realized that behind the closed doors of Fereydoun's now empty room, my mother was also taking music lessons and was learning how to play the tar. Bibi was infuriated by my mother's actions and had discussed the situation with my father. She had told him that my mother's defiant act was an insult to his manly honor.

For the first and last time, Bibi and my father, who were sworn enemies, with the excuse of protecting the integrity of their religious beliefs and their family honor, had joined forces and together had quelled the radical spirit of Houshang and my mother. Bibi, who was truly a believer, was not powerful enough to stand up to my mother, so she had solicited the help of my father. My father, who was a regular drunken patron of salons and coffee houses where the entertainment was usually live music, agreed to conspire with Bibi and to assist in her efforts.

I began attending the Fifteenth of Bahman Elementary School. Quickly, school became an entity that I loved desperately. Fereydoun had moved to Tehran and he had joined the ranks of young new poets who, through their poetry, spiced up the political gatherings of the time. The movement to nationalize the Iranian oil industry had begun to take shape. On the streets, one name was on the lips and minds of everyone: Mohammad Mossadegh.

I remember that our teachers would sometime spread carpets in the school yard, would serve tea and sweets, and invite and encourage community members to buy pieces of paper they called "national notes." Mohammad Mossadegh, the leader of the Iranian Nationalist Movement, had asked the people for financial help in achieving national goals. Mossadegh was forced to battle both the colonial powers of Britain and the supporters of the Shah, who viewed the interests of the nation and the nationalists as being in direct contradiction to their own personal interests. Despite the fact that neither my childhood contemporaries nor I were familiar with the workings of politics at that time, I do remember very well two distinct political slogans: "Death to the

Shah" and "Death to Mossadegh." It is now documented that after a short while, with the help of the American government, the slogan "Death to Mossadegh" was realized and the Shah once again managed to regain his complete and unconditional power.

Fereydoun and his intellectual contemporaries, who were of another generation, were greatly damaged by these events. The intellectual community that had gained much support and vigor from both the right and the left became depressed and hopeless. Political hopelessness had taken hold of all of the intellectuals and political activists, and active participation in political parties had become an obsolete act. As a result, the world of my childhood had become smaller. In the summers, my brother, my mother and I would travel to Tehran to visit with Fereydoun, who would take me to his gatherings, where young poets, men and women, influenced by the political developments spearheaded by Mossadegh, would disseminate hope and joy. The trips to Tehran, especially the chance to participate in the poetry readings and political gatherings with Fereydoun, remain some my most treasured childhood memories.

Despite the fact that they imprisoned Mossadegh and closed down all the political parties and organizations, it took the Iranian people a long time to become apolitical and turn into the quiet observers of the theater of politics. Families would warn their children against involvement in politics. One night my mother put on her *chador* and took my hand in search of my brother Houshang, who was attending a political meeting. Despite the fact that Houshang was no longer a child, that night my mother treated him like one, and fearful of the possibility of losing him as well, she entered the meeting and took him by the ear, forcing him home.

My mother warned that she would not allow her children to get involved in political games. She increased Houshang's allowance on the condition that he stay away from politics and go to the cinema instead. She even gave him money to buy himself a projector. With these bribes, Houshang would on occasion buy me beautiful gifts, such as sunglasses or an umbrella. These gifts were the envy of other children my age. On occasion he would take me to the cinema with him. He loved Farid el Atrash and Om Kolthoum, both Egyptian vocalists.

My mother had managed to get into debt and was forced to borrow money from a merchant from the city of Malayer, who would come to Ahvaz from time to time for business and used to lend money to those in need at high interest—a practice opposed by Islamic doctrine. My mother put up our house as collateral and came home from the notary public where the loan documents had been signed with bundles of money. But she was not able to pay back her debt or the agreed upon interest in the time allotted, so at the request of my mother, the merchant from Malayer came to Ahvaz for a meeting. During that meeting the merchant asked for my mother's hand in marriage. In return he promised to allow her full control and management of his financial affairs. My mother pointed out that she already had a husband, and the merchant assured her that he would manage to get her a divorce. "Your husband doesn't deserve you," he said. She returned home empty handed.

My mother had asked for a little more time to repay her debt, and instead she had received a marriage proposal. She declined, and a few days later the title of the house was transferred to the merchant. We became renters. This was not the first time my mother had been betrayed by men who claimed to be true Muslims. When my mother had gone for a divorce to the notary public a few years before, she had been insulted by the cleric there, who asked, "Why do you want a divorce? Do you have some lofty ideas in your head? Have you found a more manly man than Mostafa?"

After that, my mother didn't think about divorce. But she had forced my father to sign papers allowing her to get a divorce whenever she desired. My mother knew that in Islamic *sharia* law a woman, if she had enough power, she could force her husband to sign documents allowing her the legal right to a divorce. Without this, divorce remained the uncontested right of men, and women could rarely convince the cleric in charge to approve their requests for divorce.

Renting destroyed the stability of our life. The sermons during the 10-day period of *Ashura* were put to a rest. My mother's women-only gatherings came to an end. The National Opium Addicts Recovery Program, implemented by the Shah, forced Baba Taghi to quit his addiction. He had received coupons with which he could buy pills to help him kick the habit. The nightly opium smoking sessions ended. One night at dinner, we saw that the little bat that would come out every night when Baba Taghi would light up his opium had dried up and died. It turned out that the bat was addicted to opium as well, and would feed his habit from the secondhand smoke of Baba Taghi's opium. After Baba Taghi quit, the bat was forced to quit his habit of opium as well, but it seems that he was not able to do without and had gone and died. Bibi mourned the death of the bat, and blamed Baba Taghi for taking the life of an innocent creature.

The ups and downs of our family life continued. I finished elementary school and entered Nezam Vafa High School. It was rumored that the girls at our school were aloof and unduly influenced by girls from Tehran who had moved to Ahvaz. Many girls in our school were accustomed to wearing the *chador*. But we all knew that most of them did so in an effort to appease their parents. These girls would take their *chador*s off half way to school and then wear them again once they were closer. While my mother never took off her *chador*, she never asked me to wear one either.

*****

With the inauguration of the science laboratory in our school, Farah Pahlavi, thd third wife of Mohammad Reza Shah, the second ruler in the Pahlavi dynasty, entered our minds. A visit of the newly established science lab was squeezed into the queen's visit to the province of Khuzestan. On that day, Farah's face was puffy and looked tired and sickly. She was in the first few months of her pregnancy. The look of security and self-determination of a queen had not yet settled in Farah's gaze. The glow of power that was a customary part of a queen's demeanor could only be realized with her ability to give birth to a son. On the day of the inauguration of our laboratory, we could easily see and feel the fear and worry that had overtaken Farah. Provincial women and girls could relate to her situation. My mother's friends would say that if she made a vow with God to place her infant in the crib of Ali Asghar during the *Ashura* mourning festivities, God would surely bless her with a boy. Like a persistent pest, fear festered under Farah's skin, and weakness and worry were reflected in her mannerisms. Farah was afraid that she might not give birth to a boy.

The source of Farah's fear—that of a woman who holds one of the highest positions of power within an ancient country—was the same as the source of the bad luck of downtrodden rural women who had owed every ounce of their livelihoods to their poverty stricken husbands. They were afraid of losing their credibility and their livelihood if unable to bear male children. Their sense of approval and self-worth was connected to the genitals of the being that squirmed within their bellies. The people had chosen Farah as their queen, had placed a crown upon her head and hung majestic jewels from her neck, so that she could give them a son, an heir to the throne. Farah's fear was rooted in *sharia*, tradition and law—the same law, tradition and *sharia* that gave legal cover to men who took to murdering their sisters and daughters.

The constitutional law, passed in 1906, defined the monarchy as the sole right of persons from a certain family, passed on from rulers to their heirs. And according to the general penal code, those who had suffered dishonor were allowed to restore their family honor through bloodshed. This law was not based on *sharia* law; rather it had been imported directly from the French penal code. The essence of the law translated into the killing of women, with legal protections. This discriminatory law was the only such pre-revolutionary law within Iran's penal code.

Those of us who clapped in honor of Farah on that day, and who looked at her with envy, also had empathy for her and for those girls who were murdered in the outskirts of the city of Ahvaz. If she were unable to conceive a boy, she would be ousted from the glory of the palace, as if she were common trash. And had we been born male, we would have been spared much of our suffering.

The first lady's trembling hands cut the tri-colored ribbon, inaugurating our small school laboratory, the first of its kind in the province of Khuzestan. The microscopes, tubes, chemical potions, tall tables and white stools, and the little frogs, white mice and dead snakes kept in jars of alcohol, had captivated the imagination of the girls of Ahvaz. Farah quickly toured the science lab and continued on her way.

I was in my last year of high school. It was 1962 when it was announced that there would be a referendum on a six-part national plan that they called the "White Revolution." They had decided to allow women to participate in this referendum as well. This was the first time the issue of women's right to vote was addressed in Iran. The issue was brought to the fore by the highest political authority. Until this point, women, according to the law, were denied the right to vote. The referendum, and opportunity to vote, was well received by the women of Ahvaz, most of whom wore the *chador*, a symbol that often attested to their conservatism. Like slaves who had been freed, scores of women showed up at polling stations. Saying that it was an attempt to promote atheism, Bibi boycotted the vote. My mother participated in the referendum. Many of my classmates and I, too, were present at polling stations. Boys loitering on street corners would tease and harass us as we made our way to the polling stations. Mostly they would warn us that no matter how much they elevated our status, in the end, we would have to care for children. They warned that we would not accomplish much more than washing the bottoms of our children. The girls didn't pay them any mind.

In the years that followed, leading up to the revolution in 1979, the teasing and harassment changed form, and it was rumored by suppressed opposition groups that the White Revolution was, in fact, a plan drafted and supported by Americans and by the CIA. The Shah's regime, according to these rumors, was merely charged with implementing the American plan. Opposition groups working underground condemned and criticized the Shah's plan to bring women into the political arena as voters. These opposition groups undermined the Shah's effort by touting slogans in defense of Islam, under the leadership of Ayatollah Khomeini, or in defense of national interests, under the leadership of Mossadegh's supporters and friends, or in defense of the rights of the worker, under the leadership of the Tudeh party. Each saw this effort as a conspiracy against Islam, national interest or the working class. In general, they claimed that the imperialist forces of the United States, which had crushed the nationalist movement, had been the culprits. But from among the opposition groups, the words of Ayatollah Khomeini condemning the White Revolution of the Shah were most effective, and compelled revolt among the "believers," mostly merchants and seminary students. Blood baths in the cities of Tehran, Qom and Tabriz on June 5, 1963, were the result of the revolts. With the support of security forces, some of which parachuted into the scene, demonstrations at Tehran University had been quelled before they got out of hand.

I entered university studies in the area of political science and law in the academic year of 1963-1964, at a time when the revolts Tehran University students, seminary students and merchants had been violently crushed. In these years, the number of female students studying law had increased and the faculty of law was no longer a male domain. The students would demonstrate their dislike for the political status quo through poetry and literature, and leftist political thought was more accessible in the university than that of the religious opposition groups. Although political freedom and freedom of speech were nonexistent, social freedoms were increasing and interaction between the sexes was on the rise, especially in the university environment. It was commonplace for men and women to befriend one another at a university, even to start dating and fall in love, and at times get married. At the university I felt that I was living according to my mother's ideals—it had become the breeding ground of modernity. My mother wanted to ensure that I had access to what she was denied, and so I moved to Tehran in an effort to ensure that I could attend university.

My mother often recalled the thinking and words of Sheikh Fazl Allah Nouri, who was opposed to the adoption of constitutional law. Fazl Allah Nouri believed that humans did not enjoy the right to determine and set laws, and they only had an obligation to comply by God's sacred laws. My mother would warn me that Sheikh Fazl Allah Nouri had many followers who opposed the right of women to grow and improve. She was always afraid that these followers would stand in our way and prevent our progress. I would laugh at my mother. How could they stop women from progress and growth?

My mother would tell me that in ancient Persian mythology and according to the belief of some ancient religions, "Men and women were made of two branches of a rhubarb tree, and had grown identically from the same root. So identical, in fact, that neither one was greater or less than the other."

*****

From 1962 onward, women became the subject of debate and conflict between the clergy and the Shah. In summary, the following examples are relevant:

1-On the 14th of Mehr in 1341 (October 6, 1962), the cabinet approved a bill allowing elections for the establishment of provincial councils *(anjoman-haaye eyalati va velayati)* and deleted any reference to laws that denied women the right to vote. In response, the clergy launched an unprecedented opposition to women's emancipation.

2- On the 10th of Azar in 1341 (November 22, 1962), because of the pressure exerted by the clerical establishment designed to reverse women's right to vote, the Shah's regime retreated and formally announced that despite the fact that the election law on the establishment of provincial councils had been approved, allowing women the right to participate in these elections, the law in its current form was not executable.

3- On the 17th of Dey in 1341 (January 7, 1963), which happened to coincide with the 25th anniversary of the forced removal of *hejab* (veiling), a group of women held demonstrations to protest the overturning of their right to vote in the provincial council elections. The demonstrations were held in front of the office of the prime minister.

On the 6th of Bahman in 1341 (January 26, 1963), the Shah held a general referendum on the National Plan of Action, referred to as the White Revolution. Women were allowed to vote in this referendum. The plan included six subsections, as follows:

1- Land reform.
2- Nationalization of forests.
3- Sale of state-owned factories to the private sector as security for land reform.
4- Profit-sharing schemes for employees in industry.
5- Reform of electoral law to enfranchise women.
6- Creation of a literacy corps to facilitate the countrywide literacy campaign.

This marked the first occasion that women were allowed to vote nationally.

The Literacy Corps was a volunteer program designed to bring education to the rural areas of Iran, and was connected with the armed forces. Literacy Corps volunteers received initial training implemented by the armed forces and, upon completion of their tour of duty, received certain benefits.

On the 12th of Esfand in 1341 (March 3, 1963), women's presence iOn the 9th of Bahman in 1341 (January 29, 1963), it was officially announced that women could volunteer to serve in the Litn the Senate and National Assembly was officially approved, allowing women for the first time to serve in elected office.

On the 23rd of Esfand in 1341 (March 14, 1963), it was officially announced that legislation which included five articles addressing domestic disputes had been presented to the Ministry of Justice for approval.

On the 25th of Esfand in 1341 (March 16, 1963), the minister of agriculture announced that women, too, could become "petit land owners," and in this regard their rights would be the same as men's.

During this time, when the conflict and debate on women's rights had escalated, the minister of justice announced that men still maintained the sole right to divorce.

In the second half of 1963, the clerical establishment, in response to efforts to advance women's rights, specifically women's participation in the provincial council elections, organized an opposition effort. Following this effort, the clerics organized resistance to the Shah and to the influence of the United States in Iran. This resistance was led by Ayatollah Khomeini, and resulted in the bloody crackdowns on June 5, 1963. The Shah and his parliament had approved *capitulation*, which called for the surrender of U.S. citizens who had committed crimes in Iran to the American authorities and embassy in Tehran, demonstrating his complete allegiance to the United States. This act enraged the public sentiment against the Shah and the United States.

*****

While at university, I met men and I not only interacted with them freely, but also developed close friendships with some of them. I also had the opportunity to meet several leading clerics. Ayatollah Meshkat and Dr. Hassan Emami, the Friday prayer leader (Imam Jomeh) of Tehran, were professors at Tehran University's Faculty of Law. Meshkat taught religious jurisprudence, or *fiqh*, and the Friday prayer leader taught civil law. The rest of the professors focused on developments in Western law, and had studied in European and American universities.

The religious jurisprudence course included 400 first-year law students, a quarter of them female. On the first day of this class in 1962, Ayatollah Meshkat had the following to say:

> "Listen up! My course can be summarized into two topics: the sexual organs of men and the sexual organs of women. Now I will give you 10 minutes to laugh as much as you see fit. But, after that, 'til the end of the academic year, you don't have the right to laugh."

The instructor was then quiet. The young men and women, sitting next to each other, squirmed in their seats with discomfort. The men laughed out loud, and the women, even the most stylish and Western looking of them all, turned red with embarrassment. Some could not stand the discomfort and left the class for a few minutes to return only after they had regained their composure. The instructor lit a cigarette and began to introduce us to the topic of his course, Islamic jurisprudence. His eyes were bluish-green and his influential gaze kept sight of all his students' actions and behavior during the entirety of the course. I never once witnessed a difference in his treatment of men vs. women.

He responded to our questions with complete honesty. He would often leave unanswered the inquiries of a few students with religious tendencies who would try to steer Meshkat toward discussing the teachings of Ayatollah Khomeini, an opponent of the Shah. On occasion, Meshkat would warn these students that "in this university, we only have one course on religious jurisprudence and I am the one instructor of that course." Several decades later, some of those students turned out to be leading figures of the Islamic Republic. One of them, a small-framed man, was later appointed as the spokesperson for the Judiciary and the Guardian Council, where he used his influence to legitimize and push forth some of the most regressive policies and efforts designed to crackdown on the press, human rights and women's rights. He worked diligently to curtail and prevent freedom of speech and assembly. His name at the time was A'arabi, but later he appeared on the political scene as Dr. El-ham.

Dr. Emami, the Friday prayer leader, taught us civil law. He had written interpretations on the civil code, which had resulted from the constitutional period and had been approved during the reign of Reza Shah in the years 1911-1914. To date, after more than 70 years, his interpretation of the civil code remains unparalleled. Emami, who was well connected to the monarchy, would appear in public as a religious figurehead, aligned with the monarchy. He was a charismatic man who was well versed in both Western and Islamic laws. He was respectful toward young people and instead of sitting in his office he would strut around the halls of the university or sit in the courtyard, all the while willing and ready to enter into discussion with students. His robes, unlike those of other clerics who mostly dressed in dark robes, were light in color and stylish, and he had a pleasant, hopeful and kind smile. He could often be seen walking with students in the halls of the university, and many students would confide in him and seek his advice on personal matters. His behavior toward female students was without prejudice and he treated female students who wore Western-style clothing with the same respect as he did those who chose the *hejab*.

*****

At a time when political discussions would take place behind closed doors, one political figure managed to achieve notoriety and was able to propagate his seemingly religious ideas guised within an attractive and expressive prose. Jalal Al-e Ahmad[7]

---

[7] Jalal Al-e Ahmad, son of a clergyman, was born in 1923 in Tehran. As a young man, Al-e Ahmad was actively involved in the Tudeh (communist) party, especially between the years 1944 and –1948, before the party was forced underground. In the early 1950s, Al-e Ahmad was also a supporter of Mohammad Mossadegh, the leader of the Nationalist Movement. As a leading dissident in the 1950s and 1960s, he

wrote *Weststruckness*, in which he condemned all that was seemingly Western in nature, from industrial gain to the changing nature of male-female relations. SAVAK, the security forces of the Shah, in an act of idiocy and cowardice, collected all copies of this publication from bookstores and libraries. Despite its severe shortcomings and weakness, this act of censorship increased the popularity of the publication among the Iranian population, especially Iranian youth, who due to the lack of opportunities for free political participation were unable to channel their enthusiasm for change and participation through democratic institutions. The lack of freedoms, including the lack of free elections, inability to participate in political parties, lack of a free press, censorship of publications, etc., allowed for a situation in which young people were easily influenced by those professing to be intellectuals, especially those with strong writing abilities.

Quickly but in secrecy, away from the ever-present eyes of the SAVAK, *Weststruckness* was copied and distributed to every university student. In those days, *Ferdowsi*, a weekly regarded as the foremost intellectual publication, became popular among youth. The weekly, which included essays from intellectuals covering a spectrum of political leanings, was held visibly in the hands of university students as a sign of their own intellectualism. With a rolled-up copy of *Ferdowsi* in their hands and a rolled-up copy of *Weststruckness* in their pockets, away from the eyes of the SAVAK security forces, university students laid claim to their status as intellectuals.

At the same time, the Shah ordered a mosque to be built at Tehran University. Under the protection of Islam and with respect for religion, the Shah's policies sought to limit the political activities of Marxist leftists. Among the monarchists and within the SAVAK were many who were committed to the promotion of religious thought within politics. These groups especially included those who were critical of the Shah's policies, but were not in any respect revolutionary; rather they could be aptly defined as reform-oriented. Special points of contention among those promoting religious thought within politics were economic reforms and those related to women's rights and advancement of

---

wrote short stories, novels and essays criticizing the Shah's regime. Al-e Ahmad died in 1969.

women's status. These reforms contradicted what they believed to be Islamic ideals.

After successfully cracking down on the Nationalist Movement, the Shah feared all opposition. On one hand, he wanted to appease the Islamists within his own government. On the other hand, he created fear and terror among the population, warning them against political involvement and activity. While having signed human rights conventions[8], he did not allow for any political freedoms. He had come to rationalize the iron-fisted policies of the SAVAK, and warned the people that with any political opening, Soviet sympathizers, with the support of the leftist Tudeh party, would overtake the country, allowing their Russian neighbors in the north to realize their expansionist desires, and endangering Iran's independence and economic stability. The Shah referred to his Islamic and Socialist critics as "Black" and "Red" ideologues.

*****

I was busy with my own work. The cultural atmosphere of the university was much more attractive to me than that provided by the city of Ahvaz, so much so that at times I found myself unable to sleep in anticipation of what the next day held for me at the university. The rising price of oil and the boost to the economy allowed a larger number of Iranians to travel to Europe. The OPEC was set up during these years by oil producing countries, which at times, in an effort to increase the price of oil, would close production and export to European countries. Traveling to Europe was no longer the exclusive luxury of rich families, and middle-class families would also take advantage of tours to the West. In the more deprived areas of the country, however, the people would contend with their poverty and often lacked access to safe drinking water. These problems were clearly the result of indifference at the policy level, as well as bad public management.

---

[8] Universal Declaration on Human Rights (1948); U.N. Covenant on Civil and Political Rights, approved by the Shah's parliament in 1976; and U.N. Covenant on Economic, Social and Cultural Rights, approved by the Shah's parliament in 1976.

Women in urban areas who did not adhere to the *hejab* became the new fashion consumers, and relationships within the public sphere changed as a result. The large majority of women who observed the *hejab* continued to do so during this time. Many of the young girls in more traditional families, though, envied the ability of their peers to take advantage of Western dress and the style of the day. These groups, despite differences, became regular readers and fans of a new monthly called *Today's Woman (Zan-e Rooz)*. This monthly had quickly become the platform from which Western culture and the concept of equality between men and women were promoted.

After finishing my four-year undergraduate degree in law and political science at Tehran University, I began to work with *Today's Woman*. Noticing my confusion brought about by the social contradictions of the time, the editor of the monthly made arrangements for me to review the letters received by the publication. The letters were mostly sent by young girls, and were so high in volume that the staff of the paper was unable to go through them all. While reading these letters, I came to realize and understand the limitations suffered by Iranian girls within their families. I learned with great surprise that Iranian girls living in traditional and religious families were withering under the control of both mothers and fathers, and that they had come to view *Today's Woman* as an illegal item they would purchase and read away from the watchful eyes of their parents. Their desperation and longing could be compared to the desire that young intellectual students opposed to the Shah's regime had for Jalal Al-e Ahmad's *Weststruckness*.

Like the young intellectuals who would, at all costs, secretly purchase and read *Weststruckness* under the watchful eyes of the SAVAK or the Shah's secret police, these girls, who feared their fathers and even their mothers, would obtain a copy of *Today's Woman* for secret enjoyment. The letters sent to the monthly indicated that these young girls and women, largely marginalized from Iranian society, envied peers who, with the latest fashions from Paris and London, occupied the public sphere, from the streets to the cinema, to the theatre and to the work place. These girls, many from traditional families, were forbidden to join their more modern peers in the social sphere, and for this they harbored resentment. On the far-off horizon they foresaw and awaited the emergence of a savior who could free them from the strangling control of their families.

2

That savior arrived at last and taught women to free themselves of their domestic servitude. With the slogans "Death to the Shah" and "Welcome Khomeini," women were afforded the opportunity to fulfill their religious duties while taking pleasure in each other's company in the open political atmosphere, via the demonstrations that ousted the Shah and brought about the revolution of 1979. But, before that savior could arrive, there were many challenges to be faced.

In the last years of the Shah's reign, Iran had come closer to ensuring equal rights between men and women. With the Shah's orders in this respect, the subject of women's rights was transformed into an issue that was open for discussion. This had of course become an excuse for opposition groups who, cloaked under the guise of their opposition to the regime, had managed to conceal their patriarchal mindsets and had prevented the natural progression of discussions on women's rights. Opposition groups—whether Islamists, nationalists or Marxists, and despite their particular allegiances—would ridicule the rights that the Shah had afforded women. They often criticized these efforts through their underground and expatriate publications. They labeled efforts to promote women's rights as marginally important and relevant, and claimed that these efforts were designed to detract from the importance of the real issues at hand. These groups believed that women's gains should not be defended, and they pretended that the supporters of the Shah wanted to focus attention on the issue of sexual relations between men and women as a strategy to distract the public from the issue of political repression. Even the adoption of the Family Law, which provided some legal safeguards for women on issues of divorce and child custody, was often labeled and criticized as an effort to promote prostitution and loosen morality.

The issue of women's rights was indeed an area upon which the nationalists and the Marxists agreed with their Islamic counterparts. In addition, the masses of women were kept largely unaware of developments on this front. In reality, the Shah, too, did not believe in the equality of women and men, but realized that it was difficult to deny educated women their basic human rights. As a result, he had appointed his sister, Ashraf Pahlavi, to spearhead efforts on behalf of women. Because of her active role in quelling opposition movements designed to oust her brother, Ashraf Pahlavi was hated by political groups. As a result, educated women, who feared being accused of conspiring with Ashraf or supporting her ideas, were reluctant to take advantage of the opening public and social space that resulted from more progressive policies, and were even more reluctant to enter the debate on women's rights.

On the other hand, the men working with the Shah, who controlled the main decision-making bodies and venues, would oppose policies designed to improve women's lives. In this respect, they agreed with opposition groups and would provide a variety of excuses designed to prevent women's advances. They claimed that Iranian society was wholly unable and unprepared to absorb changes in the status of women, and that the religious leadership in Qom and Mashad would be infuriated by legal measures designed to advance women's rights. At most, they worked to appease the female members of the legal commissions with whom they served. Some of these men, however, supported amendments and laws addressing women's issues and legal rights at the personal urging of Ashraf Pahlavi. In other words, the Shah's men realized that disobeying Ashraf would risk their positions, and so they were forced to give in to her demands.

Ashraf and her brother were twins. They had been nurtured in the same environment. One twin, with the support of the constitution, and in accordance with the advantages afforded him by virtue of his sex, had been crowned as the ruler of Iran; and the other twin, having not been born male, had been denied the crown. Ashraf was willing to partake in any action or plot designed to ensure her position of power—a position directly linked to her brother's ability to hold on to the throne. Her struggles were in essence a struggle against her fate as a woman. Ashraf Pahlavi did not, however, enjoy much popularity. Opposition groups hated her and the Shah's men feared her. Despite these realities, she had taken on the responsibility of implementing some of the royal orders within the Shah's administration in favor of women's rights.

*****

The presence of women in the more sensitive areas – such as in ministries, on court benches as judges, as members of parliament, the diplomatic core or the police force in the last years of the Shah's reign – not only accelerated social developments, but also created a great deal of conflict and tension. The opposition groups viewed the Shah as an American puppet, and as a result opposed any political strategy adopted by the Shah that could spur social and political change. At the same time, these groups took advantage of the Iranian public's collective memory, which resented the Shah's regime for crushing the Nationalist Movement that claimed as its achievement success in nationalizing Iran's oil industry. Eventually the Shah, with support from the American government, had rendered the Nationalist Movement powerless and had placed its leader, Mohammad Mossadegh, under house arrest. Opposition leaders did not want to allow the Shah any glory and worked to undermine his power and strength, and as a result they vehemently fought even the policies designed to promote women's rights, fearing that they would allow the Shah some advantage. Talented and qualified women, relying on pre-revolutionary social freedoms, could have taken the initiative to create and support civil organizations aimed to empower and promote women's rights and a women-oriented agenda, within the framework of development plans—an issue within the mandate of the government. However, because they feared being labeled by opposition groups as supporters of the Shah, they refused to take advantage of these opportunities.

As a result, the majority of women—especially those who lived in religious and patriarchal households – remained largely unaware of the importance of the Shah's policies that for whatever reason sought to advance women's rights, and were not able to take advantage of these new opportunities. The information ministries of the Shah failed to ensure the freedoms necessary for a fruitful debate on social issues, in particular women's issues.

Instead, these groups focused their public relations campaigns on forcing political prisoners associated with opposition leaders to appear on television and inform the Iranian public of the threat of the "Red advancement," meaning advancement of Marxist opposition groups, or the "Black advancement," meaning advancement of religious opposition groups. These television shows, which had come to be largely referred to as the SAVAK shows, promoted an impression of the Shah's public relations team within information ministries as stupid and ignorant, which in essence created a sense of political disillusionment and hopelessness among the Iranian public.

When Khosrow Golsorkhi, an intellectual and poet charged with endangering national security, cried during his televised court proceedings and—instead of confessing to wrongdoing and regretting his opposition to the Shah's regime—emphasized the need to continue the resistance based on Shiite mythological beliefs that called for defiance of tyranny, it became clear to the Iranian public that a coalition between leftists and Islamists was indeed a possible solution for effectively opposing the Shah's regime. The Iranian public, both in secret and in public, empathized with Golsorkhi's predicament. He and another of his contemporaries, Keramat Daneshian, were sentenced to death after the broadcast of their trial and killed by a firing squad in 1975.

This development acted as a catalyst in returning the Iranian public to the political scene, after its withdrawal in August of 1953. Khosrow Golsorkhi was a popular journalist, poet and intellectual, and the Iranian public witnessed his tearful eyes, filled with love for his people, and cried along with him. Before Golsorkhi's execution by a firing squad, other opposition leaders, many of whom were engaged in armed conflict against the regime, were charged with disrupting the peace, entering government buildings and robbing banks, and had been either killed by the regime during conflict or executed by a firing squad. After Golsorkhi's execution, the television shows and other executions continued. But Golsorkhi's televised trial and his execution were viewed differently by the Iranian public, which realized that the Shah's regime would not tolerate poets and journalists. In response, the Iranian public realized that they could not tolerate a regime that treated its intellectuals in such a cruel and inhumane manner, and awaited the opportunity to rid itself of its government.

Policies addressing women's rights that had been approved and promoted by the Shah's regime were resisted by the people. Religious families relied on the words and interpretations of their religious leaders and Islamic jurists in defining their own beliefs and values. These religious leaders opposed modern beliefs and values, which were promoted by the Shah in the form of the legal measures and national development plans addressing women's rights.

After the bloody events of June 5, 1963, resistance of the Shah's reforms continued behind closed doors, in homes, during religious festivities and under the guise of Koranic studies and meetings. In the absence of a strong civil society sector, these gatherings were able to link together like a string of beads to create an effective and major political development, based upon religious belief. Ayatollah Khomeini's audiotapes and pamphlets, seeking to lead this emerging movement, were broadly distributed in secrecy. Khomeini had been forced into exile, first to Turkey and then to Iraq. His followers had monetary resources, which they collected in his name from traditionalist merchants in the bazaar. But they had not managed to attract university students as followers. The university was generally the breeding ground for nationalists and leftist opposition groups that resisted the religious leadership.

This division was disrupted by Dr. Ali Shariati[1], an Islamic scholar who had studied in the UK. In his position as a critic of the political status quo, he was able to awaken the excitement of

---

[1] Dr. Ali Shariati was born in 1933 in Mazinan, a suburb of Mashad, Iran. He completed his elementary and high school education in Mashad and later attended the Teachers' Training College. Shariati graduated from college in 1960 and pursued graduate studies in France. His Islamic revival focused on enlightening the masses, especially youth, among whom he gained great popularity and a substantive following. Shariati was imprisoned by the regime of the Shah on two occasions and remained under pressure, unable to lecture or publish, after he was released for the second time in 1975. He traveled to England and was found dead three weeks later in his apartment on June 19, 1977. It is widely believed that he was murdered by the SAVAK.

the Iranian youth. His poetic prose about believers and Shiites built on the subconscious beliefs of the Iranian public and ignited fervor in the minds and hearts of young people. The humble home of Fatemeh, the daughter of the Prophet Mohammad, became the source of Dr. Shariati's political inspiration. Calling young people to action, he criticized traditional conservative religious leaders and claimed that it was not appropriate to just sit still and wait for Mahdi, the 12th Imam (the Shiite Messiah), and for judgment day. Rather he claimed that the people should take the lead in creating the conditions necessary for the emergence of the Shiite Messiah. Shariati worked to modernize and make tangible the myth of Fatemeh for young women and girls. He placed great emphasis on this female myth and in so doing made her story attractive to scores of women. The oratory aptitude of Dr. Shariati, who wore a tie and looked and acted Western, was mesmerizing.

The Shah's SAVAK was at first delighted by the emergence of Dr. Shariati, hoping that with his charisma he could aid the proliferation of Islamic ideas, and with his criticism of the religious leaders he would be able to dissuade educated youth from joining the Marxist movement. As a result, the SAVAK allowed Dr. Shariati to set up his headquarters in Hosseinieh Ershad[2] and promote his religious thinking in a modern language that was attractive to youth. In the absence of independent political parties and organizations, young people flocked to Hosseinieh Ershad in hopes of finding an alternative to fleeing their homeland or succumbing to the Shah's orders, which called for membership in the one and only government sponsored and supported political party, the Rastakhiz Party. Dr. Shariati injected the Shiite mythology with the attractive elements of Marxism, and as a result transformed the educated youth – who had become disillusioned with politics but longed for genuine participation in the political process – into a political force supported by religion and capable of altering the political order.

---

[2] Hosseinieh Ershad is a community center and, although attached to a mosque, is open for lectures by non-clerical Islamic scholars. Many key figures of the revolution used this center as a venue for delivering speeches, including Dr. Shariati. Hosseinieh Ershad owes its reputation to Shariati. After the revolution, Hosseinieh Ershad attracted many moderate Islamic thinkers.

Shariati gained notoriety in the last decade of the Pahlavi rule at a time when Iran, as a result of increased access to higher education, was faced with the emergence of new social groups. A larger number of women had gained access to the workforce. At the same time, Iran was facing modern social issues such as urbanization and Westernization, and the emergence of new phenomena such as industrialization and the stock market, all of which demonstrated Iran's reliance on international powers. Within Iran, the new intellectuals and secular thinkers had never observed anything in Islam capable of responding to these developments, except calls for isolation from the modern world. Islam had not adapted itself to the new world order, and it could even be said that it played a negative role by directing attention to judgment day, and that its silence guaranteed the survival of an oppressive regime. Iranian youth, both Islamists and intellectuals, found a revolutionary response in Shariati that was not only based on the Shiite tradition, but also responded to the Iranian zeal. He invited these young people to revolt and asked them to adapt their earthly existence to be in line with Islamic teaching. He was able to attract a young generation of Iranians who were not ideological and to transform a state of indifference and inaction into one of active youth working for the revolution.

Two decades after the Iranian revolution of 1979, Iranian scholars described Jalal Al-e Ahmad and Ali Shariati as intellectuals opposed to modernization. As Iranian scholar and intellectual Ramin Jahanbegloo explained, for example, in a December 2004 interview with Radio Farda:

The third generation of Iranian intellectuals was largely opposed to modernity. Jalal Al-e Ahmad and Ali Shariati were two pragmatic thinkers of this generation of intellectuals who were opposed to both the idea of modernity as well as the Pahlavis, and promoted the idea of a return to self and to ethnic identities. Their importance lies in the fact that they played a role in laying the foundation of the revolution.

During my youth, I would attend Dr. Shariati's lectures. On occasion, I would be influenced by his teachings and accept his ideas. But the minute I discussed his ideas at home, my mother, recounting her own experiences and the experiences of other women, would dissolve any notion in me that had entertained the compatibility of religion and politics. She would explain that the

foundation of politics could not be based on a religious foundation. If it were, she claimed, a traditional conservative religious
leader would take control.

Modernity had become an integral part of my mother's being.
Despite the fact that she had not had the opportunity to attend
modern schools or university, and was a housewife who had
never traveled to the West, she had come to understand in her
own way the modern and Western worlds, and she was unwilling
to be influenced by the attractive political discourse of the day
and abandon her own understanding of the world.

*****

My marriage to a journalist disrupted my social life. My husband, Siamak Pourzand, encouraged me to take up writing. At
the time, I was employed by the government at the Social Welfare Organization and was clerking for the court. Abbas
Pahlavan, the editor in chief of a weekly called *Ferdowsi*, expressed interest in publishing my writings. As a result, I quickly
integrated myself and gained a reputation among cultural activists, who under the oppressive regime of the Shah had learned
well the art of self-censorship. The articles I published in the
weekly *Ferdowsi*, and other publications, can be broadly classified into two distinct areas: articles addressing social issues
within Iran, and political articles addressing international developments.

The first cadre of articles highlighted and analyzed the cultural and social poverty of women within the context of familial
and social relations, and the second cadre of articles addressed
and analyzed the impediments to democracy in dictatorships.
Despite the fact that I was in contact with a variety of opposition
groups and enjoyed friendships with a number of opposition
leaders, I never became active in political movements and organizations. I was in love with writing. The political situation of
the country, at the time, was darkly and negatively reflected in
all my writings. Given the realities of the time and of my life,
involvement in revolutionary movements and opposition groups,
heroism, and direct confrontation with political power brokers—
which could easily destroy my life—were not options.

I felt that I could be more effective in the long run if I concentrated on my writing, which I had come to master, and worked to expose social dynamics through this venue. I did not feel rushed in my efforts to create change. I understood the complexities and difficulties of Iranian society. I believed that a revolutionary spirit would not afford me my desired results, and that heroism and revolutionary characteristics were not a part of my nature. The Cold War, neocolonialism, the Vietnam War, the emergence of Abdul Nasser's nationalism in Egypt, Che Guevara, the Six-Day War between Israel and Arab nations, the military coups that brought about political changes in the new governments in Latin America, the demonstrations of Western youth in the 1960s, and many other international developments had occupied the attention and time of Iranian youth engaged in writing. These writers empathized with the hungry in Africa, Palestinian victims, the Viet Cong, and the plight of the American Indians, but were not allowed to write about the increasing political disenchantment and the anger of the Iranian people.

*****

The closed political atmosphere contributed to the ever-increasing anger of Iranians. This was a sign of the storm that awaited Iran, but the Shah and his supporters did not want to acknowledge it. An increasing number of women, mostly young and urban, had chosen a particular form of the *hejab* that was political, and not necessarily a testament to their religious beliefs. *Hejab* had become a symbol through which these young women could express their opposition to the Shah. Even young women in the northern parts of Tehran, which was home to the most modern and Western-oriented social groups, could be seen wearing the *hejab*, at schools and in social gathering places. This new *hejab* was very different from my mother's or my grandmother's *hejab*. This *hejab* was a reactionary response objecting to the White Revolution and to the changing legal status of women, and demonstrated an approval for Ayatollah Khomeini's orders from Najaf and the poetic discourse offered by Dr. Ali Shariati to Iranian women and girls, who weren't necessarily brought up in religious, extremist or traditional families.

Nevertheless, these young people suffered from the absence of democratic institutions and organizations through which they could express their demands in a peaceful and constructive manner. A government that could not, through the facilitation of independent organizations and political parties, establish a relationship with the people also did not take the signs of discontent seriously, and could not understand that the *hejab* of young, urban, modern and non-religious girls was quickly transforming into a political symbol. The Shah's men were not akin to problem solving and believed that while the SAVAK was keeping abreast of developments in the Iranian political scene, nothing would change.

In the days when issues concerning the female sex were at the core of the policies of the Shah and his opposition, when both wanted to use women's feelings and needs to strengthen their own political power, I became a mother.

My daughter Lily was born in 1975. My experience of motherhood was bittersweet. The joy of motherhood was greater than any happiness I had ever felt. At the same time, motherhood forced me to reduce my social activities. It became extremely difficult for me to write during this time. The long nights and interrupted sleep patterns that resulted from having a newborn in the house had disrupted my life's order. My mother helped as much as she could, but it was not enough. Slowly I learned the fine art of balancing motherhood, writing and full-time employment. This was a fragile balance that was largely out of my control, and easily disrupted at Lily's whim. A bout with diarrhea, an occasional sore throat or an infection was enough to stop me in my tracks and force me to be a full-time mother, taking away my ability to write or to go to work. I was a 30-year-old mother with a wide spectrum of social relations, in a politically sensitive time that witnessed the fall of the monarchy.

The cafés of Tehran were good gathering places for journalists and social and cultural activists. The new intellectuals of Iran, who had surfaced and grown with the emergence of Nima Yushij's new poetry, were now defining themselves nightly in Tehran's cafés. The intellectuals of the day, who after the coup de tat against Mosaddegh on August 19, 1953, had come to be known as unified in their outlook, criticized the Shah's regime, not directly, but through the use of metaphors. They portrayed the political atmosphere of Iran as dark and restrictive through their poetry, short stories, novels, paintings, music and other works. Metaphors, as opposed to direct attacks, were the preferred strategy of the intellectual community, as they provided some level of immunity against attacks from the SAVAK.

Marxist ideology largely impacted the thinking of the new intellectualism in Iran, and it was this ideology that was reflected in poetry and art. Writers, poets and artists who did not include a criticism of the political status quo in their works were sharply criticized within intellectual circles, accused of not understanding their own calling and of supporting the regime. This pattern was similar to that which was set out in the field of women's rights. Just as harassments based in ideology prevented progress in attaining women's rights and improving women's conditions, artists who did not want to combine politics and factionalism with art quickly became marginalized, and the definition of the arts narrowed. Those who felt that the arts should serve political causes designed to address social injustices and class differences, and who criticized the regime, quickly gained social and political fame and positions of notoriety. The bar at Hotel Marmar, located on Fisher Abad Avenue, had become the hangout for these artists-turned-critics. Young and old, those engaged in and interested in contemporary art and literature would gather nightly in these hangouts, just as scores of young people, in the absence of political parties and civil organizations, attended the lectures of Dr. Shariati at Hosseinieh Ershad. At the artistic and intellectual gatherings at the bar of Hotel Marmar, they drank alcohol while sharing with one another their experiences of resistance and their artistic passions.

On occasion, these gatherings included heated exchanges between some of the better-known figures. On one occasion, Dr. Gholamhossein Saedi, whose plays I read regularly, criticized me for focusing too much on women's issues and not addressing the root causes of social and political problems. He discussed with great admiration one of my articles that highlighted the situation of American Indians, and encouraged me to focus on such topics more often and forgo the issue of women's rights. Focusing on women's rights, he said, demonstrated undue influence from new and old imperialist powers on my reporting ability.

In those years, I felt that the political, religious and intellectual tendencies toward dictatorial rule created a sense of disillusionment among active youth, or otherwise pushed them toward extremism. It took a long time before I could recover from Dr. Gholamhossein Saedi's words and observations and return to my own passions.

*****

During such a sensitive time, the Shah's Ministry of Information, which was charged with regulating the press, published a list forbidding certain writers and journalists from writing. Those blacklisted also included independent writers with no connection to political opposition groups. This further obstructed the political process and negatively influenced even those who wrote for official publications supported by the state. Publications were instructed not to publish the works of blacklisted writers.

My social life as a mother was slowly losing its appeal. The press was not an ideal forum for the expression of ideas. The Women's Organization of Iran, headed by Mahnaz Afkhami, who later became the minister of women's affairs, invited me to take part in the low literacy legal education program for women, and I accepted. At first, we were supposed to convene educational classes in parks and in public spaces that could be easily accessed by women. But we were told that the SAVAK was opposed to the use of public spaces for the purpose of teaching women their legal rights, as it would infuriate religious leaders and incite their followers into direct confrontation with women participating in the classes. As a result of this warning, these courses were convened in the offices of the Women's Organization. During my cooperation with the Organization and as a result of my work in the legal education program, I realized that the National Women's Organization was being managed by a number of well-qualified women with great expertise. But working with the support of Ashraf Pahlavi hindered their ability to connect with a wide spectrum of women from different social classes. In other words, they were not successful in attracting the participation of women in their political and legal programs, which included sophisticated discussions based on principals of development and growth.

The National Organization for Women was, however, very successful in its family health and planning programs. Women from lower economic classes linked up with the Organization's various branches throughout the country to benefit from programs offering free pregnancy prevention services and formula for newborn babies. Much of the progress in reforming the Family Law, and other laws that sought to advance the status of women, resulted from the collective efforts of the Women's Organization and the contribution of collaborating lawyers.

In 1977, I resigned from the Social Welfare Organization and decided to take the bar exam. Amir Abbas Hoveyda, who had become prime minister after Hassan Ali Mansour, was terrorized by a religious political group called the Martyrs of Islam in 1964. As a result, his 13-year tenure as prime minister came to an end. Human rights organizations, which were on occasion allowed to visit Iran, were alarmed by the situation of political prisoners and exposed other human rights violations by the Shah's regime as well. The international press increasingly criticized the political atmosphere in Iran – a trend that had begun in 1975. As a result, the Shah was forced to appoint a new prime minister. Despite these political changes, writers and the press remained under scrutiny and pressure.

The political environment remained closed until, under pressure from U.S. President Jimmy Carter, the Shah was forced to open it up. At the same time, national developments added to a sense of dissatisfaction and increased the discord within Iran. Religious opponents of the regime took to the streets in demonstrations. These protesters were inflamed by a letter published, at the orders of officials at the Security and Information ministries, in the daily *Ettelaat*, which projected a disrespectful tone toward the exiled Khomeini. These demonstrations, which took place mostly in the more conservative and religious cities of Qom, Mashad, Isfahan and Tabriz, resulted in a large number of deaths. On the rise since 1977, these oppositional demonstrations and acts of resistance made the claims of the Shah, who pegged Iran as a stable island in the unstable Middle East, seem ridiculous. At first the smaller opposition groups joined together in an effort to create a unified front. Ayatollah Khomeini was forced out of Najaf and took refuge in France. As a result, opposition leaders traveled regularly to France to visit with Khomeini, who

commonly ordered the Iranian people to organize and join demonstrations against the Shah's regime.

In a broad effort to organize an opposition movement, the
mosques turned into centers for political organization and activism. The nationalists, Marxists, Islamic-socialists and other opposition groups accepted the leadership of Ayatollah Khomeini.
The more open atmosphere pushed the press to expose corruption with the goal of arousing the public. As a result, the press,
recently freed from the oppressive measures of the Shah's regime, did not sufficiently address the need for a unified system
that could replace the existing government. The Shah's security
forces slowly weakened as a result of the increased activism of
opposition groups, and books that had long been banned from
publication began to emerge with blank white covers and were
sold on street corners. These included publications by the Nationalist Front, the Freedom Front, Marxist groups, and books by
opposition leaders such as Dr. Shariati.

Revolutionary demonstrations were on the rise. I vigilantly
observed the various developments during this time, but it
seemed that a force greater than that of public developments prevented me from joining these groups. On occasion, I would stare
at a group of revolutionaries gathered in a store or at a café, and I
felt as though an immense glass was separating me from them.
Everyone wanted the Shah to leave and seemed to claim that any
replacement would result in improvement of the current situation.

In line with his other orders for public demonstrations, Ayatollah Khomeini ordered a strike for the press. A few writers and
journalists felt that this order was counterproductive and decided
against it. I was one of the journalists who crossed the picket
line. Along with a small number of colleagues, we published
Ferdowsi, which had been banned at the order of the Shah for
some time. In the few issues of *Ferdowsi* that were published
during the press strike, we included several pieces by Dr. Mahdi
Bahar. In his writings and in an effort to inform the Iranian public, Bahar tried to explain and expose the type of government
that Ayatollah Khomeini had advocated – one with a Supreme
Leader at its helm.

This effort, despite its wisdom, was unfortunately too late,
and as a result the articles of Dr. Mahdi Bahar, like many other

warnings about what awaited Iran, were lost in the excitement of the revolution. Those who warned and those who tried to lead the course of events in a different direction were the first to suffer the consequences of their actions and became the subject of great criticism.

As for me, I came to be known for disobeying the orders of the leader of the revolution, and for not taking part in the press strike I was accused of opposing the revolution. This act forever overshadowed and darkened my revolutionary record. The press syndicate accused me of counterrevolutionary activities – an accusation that was published in their bulletin and was placed in a file with my name on it. Despite its cooperation with the revolution and its sympathies for revolutionaries, the syndicate was accused of cooperation with the Shah's regime, and quickly lost its revolutionary credentials.

The Shah left Iran and Ayatollah Khomeini returned from France. It was an eventful winter for Iran, and people from all social and economic groups joined the revolutionary movement and took part in demonstrations across the nation. During this time, when the Islamic Revolution had not officially come to power, Ayatollah Shariatmadari, who enjoyed a great following and was regarded as one of the better known religious leaders, announced in an interview that according to Islam, women were not suited to be judges. The same period was witness to the first attempt at segregating men and women in the public sphere.

Ayatollah Khomeini, after a broad and joyful reception by the Iranian people, chose Tehran as his place of residence and, despite the fact that he had promised to reside in Qom and refrain from involvement in politics, allowing politicians to take up that task, he took a leadership position within the capital city. On February 3, 1980, Khomeini hosted separate visits from men and women who wanted to pay him their respects. This event was the impetus for later policies that sought to segregate men and women in offices and other public spaces, sometimes through the use of black canvas curtains.

Through a precise and well-planned strategy, Ayatollah Khomeini was asked to comment on the Family Law, approved in 1974 by the Shah. The intent was to label all legal measures designed to improve the status of women during the Shah's regime as un-Islamic and in contradiction to *sharia* law, rendering these measures ineffective. Those opposed to women's advancement first targeted legal gains, which resulted in denying women the rights they had gained with respect to divorce and as guardians of their children. But Khomeini never reversed women's right to vote, which was provided to them under the Shah. With this clever strategy, Khomeini was able to mobilize Iranian women's vote in support of the establishment of the Islamic Republic.

In early March of 1979, Ayatollah Khomeini, in a lecture given during a visit with Islamic jurists and seminary students in Qom, asked women employed within the government sector to observe the Islamic *hejab* within their workplaces. While many revolutionary decisions opposed women's rights during this period, the leader of the Islamic Republic's proposition to enforce the *hejab* created much tension and conflict within the political arena. The majority of women who chose not to observe the *hejab*, but who had nonetheless participated in demonstrations that brought about the revolution, made up the first group to oppose the Islamic regime. On March 8, 1979, women gathered in front of the judiciary building to object to forced *hejab*. They chanted and yelled slogans against the proposition.

I was one of those activists who made my objections to forced *hejab* for women known on that day. In fact, I would identify the events of March 8, International Women's Day, as the starting point of my activities in support of women's rights and human rights within the Islamic regime. This effort, along with many others spearheaded by women in the early days of the revolution, faced harsh crackdowns. Women took to the streets to demonstrate against forced *hejab* and the retraction of the rights accorded them through the Family Law, and for their right to serve as judges. They faced retaliations by a group called Hezbollah (or the Party of God), which was armed with insults and threats, forcing the protestors to disperse.

These oppositional acts were followed by broad arrests of women. Additionally, many of those opposed to these policies were dismissed from their professions, sometimes from positions they had held for several years. The arrests and dismissals became a lesson for many women, who decided against public protest in an effort to hold on to their jobs and to stay out of prison. I, too, chose this path. It was important for me to retain my law license, which I had only managed to obtain three months prior to the revolution. My license transformed into an idealistic symbol for me, which I never relinquished, and maintained sometimes at high costs. The revolutionary fervor had not penetrated me, and now I was witness to the revolutionary actions of a group of merciless and patriarchal men who were pushing forth the objectives of an Islamic regime. I realized that I was not capable of directly confronting these forces, and despite this reality, I decided against migrating from Iran and instead chose the tumultuous state of affairs in my own country.

3

I pushed back a canvas curtain. The day before there was no sign of the curtain. The day before there was one main entrance to the judiciary building. On this day the pages of history had turned. The women's entrance had been separated from the men's entrance. A few women were sitting behind the curtain that marked the women's entrance. They had been put in charge of inspecting the *hejab* and the makeup of women entering the Judiciary Building. One of them placed her hand behind my neck. She felt around and said, "Sister, you can't enter the building looking like this. Cover your neck." I opened my scarf and tied it around my neck so that it would cover my neck fully. The woman was pleased. But her colleague did not allow me to enter.

"You are wearing perfume," she said. "Go outside and fan yourself in the fresh air, then come back. Perhaps the fresh air will take away the smell of your perfume a bit."

I obliged. I pushed back the curtain and exited the building. A crowd had gathered in front of the men's entrance, but there were no signs of a curtain. A few of the men were removing their ties and placing them in their pockets or briefcases. I passed them by. I felt strange around them. This was not how I had felt before. This was not how I felt yesterday. That damned curtain had disoriented me. I saw a lawyer who was walking toward the entrance of the Judiciary Building. As it had always been customary, I waived at my colleague. He gave me a bitter look. I moved toward him so that perhaps, by talking to him, I could relieve this strange and alien feeling. I said hello and stretched out my hand in an attempt to shake his. Again, he looked at me bitterly and did not reach for my hand. Blood rushed to my face as my hand remained suspended in mid-air. Embarrassed and regretful, I felt my face burning. I felt humiliated, and my male colleague, with his bitter stare, forced me to understand that on that very day, a page of history had turned. He wanted to make me understand. It was as if he were saying with his eyes, "Yes, on this day … what are you thinking?" It dawned on me that all our values had turned upside down. Now touching, even a simple handshake, between men and women who were not close relatives was forbidden. It was against Islamic *sharia* law to touch an unrelated man.

I remembered that I had come outside so that the fresh air could alleviate the scent of my perfume, which had so bothered the female guard. I started to walk. I stopped in front of the statue of the Angel of Justice, which had stood atop the Judiciary Building for half a century. In its shadow I began to calm down. The angel still remained. This thought consoled me.

Again, I pushed back the canvas curtain. This time the women allowed me to enter the building. I entered. It was obvious that I had lost my self-confidence. It seemed to me that everyone was looking me over. I felt as if everyone wanted to give me a warning. Familiar faces of men I knew turned away from me. It was as if the canvas curtain, despite being hung only that day, had succeeded in segregating all of us from one another. .

On the days that followed, the number of curtains separating men and women increased. . On this side of the curtains women had become ugly and looked unhappy, and on the other side it seemed that the men had grown beards. It was as if the curtain had a problem with smiles, with modesty, with cleanliness or with scents of perfume. There was no sign of the pretty, well-dressed women and girls, who as court clerks, lawyers and judges once occupied the halls of the judiciary. The employees of the judiciary, who once would welcome the young clerks with encouraging smiles and who would show respect by standing as women entered the room, had become morose and frowned at those who came to the judiciary for a chance to learn their trade and to gain expertise in their profession. Fear of speaking with, looking at, and occupying the same space as women had turned the whites of the men's eyes a shade of yellow. Why had this happened? Why did the emphasis on Islamic ideology evoke fear to reflect in the eyes of men for years following the 1979 revolution? Why had joy deserted the faces of both men and women? Without knowing the answers to my many questions, I wandered the halls, frowning and lethargic.

I entered a courtroom designated for divorce proceedings. The presence of an Islamic cleric had overwhelmed the room. He sat there in his black turban and black cloak. This cleric later became the head of the family court, addressing family disputes. I moved closer to his desk –which I was accustomed to doing – so that I could inquire about the case of my client, a woman seeking a divorce from her husband. Without looking at the case file, he pushed it aside.

"If you want a divorce, come back tomorrow. I don't have the time today," he said.

I explained that I was not seeking a divorce, but rather that I was a lawyer requesting that he provide me his decision on the case in writing so that I could file the decision with the court. He frowned, as if I had trespassed on his territory, as if I had threatened his power.

"I don't care if you are a lawyer. Where is your client?" he said.

"She is employed and she can't accompany me to the court on a daily basis," I replied.

"So, the one who is seeking a divorce is you, not her," he screamed. "You are trying to fill your pocket with her money. Leave immediately."

Before I could utter a response, the court clerk, a bearded man, moved toward me. "Follow me, sister," he commanded. I obeyed. Outside the courtroom he provided me with advice. He told me that the country had become Islamic. Men were now both lawyers and judges. He explained that if I wanted them to allow me into the courtroom, I should always go to the court with my client. "Don't speak," he advised. "Let your client speak, and if she insists and even if she cries, the judge will be more sympathetic. And be mindful of your *hejab*. The judge is not joking. He is serious about these issues and is a tough man."

I bowed my head and like a lamb I left the court of a cleric-turned-judge. When I arrived at home, I could see that my mother had prepared a soup for lunch, using the kerosene heater. I had no appetite. I knew that my mother had prepared the meal with great difficulty. She asked me how I felt and I responded, "So-so," with a nod of the head.

"God is great. Why don't you eat something?" She asked.

"Where is Lily?" I inquired.

"She has gone with her cousins to a demonstration."

"What demonstration?"

"I'm not sure. I think they are supposed to burn the American flag."

"Why did you allow her to go?" I asked, alarmed.

"She wanted to go. I can't confine her to the house. She has more fun with her cousins. Her father is depressed. You can't sleep or eat. She will suffer this way. Demonstrations are an outlet for young people these days. Lily will have fun. Don't worry."

I realized that my mother was right. It was better that my daughter spend time with her cousins, so that she would not be subjected to our depressed faces.

My experience at the judiciary continued to be a negative one. I could not sleep at night. I lay awake thinking about how I would have to go back to that hellhole in the morning. I thanked God that the new judges did not know that I was the same Mehrangiz Kar who published her articles during the Shah's time. I thanked God that the name on my license to practice law was "Mehrangiz Kar-Kheiran" rather than "Mehrangiz Kar." I thanked God that the new judges did not know that I was the same writer whose picture, with no *hejab* and short hair styled after the singer Googoosh, regularly appeared alongside her articles. I thanked God that my father had chosen the name Kar-Kheiran as our family name and that my brother, during his years as a poet, had signed his poetry as Fereydoun Kar, and had allowed me to use the same shortened version of our name in my own writings.

The new judges were extremely upset at the continued presence of lawyers in their courts. They viewed the courts as their own property, to which they had an inherent right—a right they had been denied as a result of the Constitutional Revolution, and especially during the reign of Reza Shah who, due to the efforts of the legal scholar Davar and later through the presence and cooperation of lawyers who had studied law in Iran and Europe, had taken the courts out of the domain of the clerics. Lawyers were among the first to realize that the desire to regain control of the court system was one of the major factors contributing to the Islamic revolution. They witnessed first hand the behavior of these clerics and realized quickly that the ideas of these revolu-

tionary clerics were similar to those of Fazlollah Noori, a prominent cleric who opposed the Constitutional Revolution. They
came to understand quickly that the revolutionary clerics and
judges were intent on regaining all that was taken from them
during the Constitutional Revolution of 1906.

First, the courts were used as a tool through which clerics
could exert their power. Later, the concept of "ordaining good
and forbidding evil," or *"al-amr bi al-ma'ruf wa al-nahy al-
munkar,"*[1] was used effectively by the clerical regime to ensure
its survival. The curtains were a sure testament to the fact that
they were preparing themselves to implement an atmosphere in
which the concept of "ordaining good and forbidding evil" was
dominant, and that social freedoms would be quickly and severely restricted.

These new judges would refuse to work with me every time I
entered the judiciary. As a result, I didn't feel justified in charg-
ing my clients. I had been too daring in taking on these cases.
The judges, it seemed, wanted to ridicule and belittle me. With
the passing of time, the number of lawyers working with the judiciary declined. Many of them shut down their practices. Others
entered into deals with power brokers in an effort to retain their
positions. Many female lawyers gave up their practices and
chose to stay home or leave the country. For many, forced *hejab*
was unbearable. I could not follow in their footsteps for several
reasons. My legal practice, which had only begun when I passed
the bar three months before the revolution, was my only source
of income. I had to support my family with this income. My
mother, my grandmother, my husband and my daughter all relied

---

[1] The obligation of ordaining the good and forbidding the evil is an
uncompromising Islamic principle. In the Islamic Republic, Sharia has
become a legal means to intrude violently into the lives of the people
and oppress them. The imperative of ordaining the good and forbidding
evil is used to control women's *hejab*, gatherings, associations, parties,
weddings, dating and the consumption of alcoholic beverages. Numerous inspection agencies believe they have the right to invade the lives
of private individuals and attack their personal preferences. Such inva-
sions are, of course, justified by the imperative of ordaining the good
and forbidding evil, as stated in Article 8 of the Constitution, which
grounds the laws governing the rights and duties of security forces and
police. See Kadivar, Mohsen, *Islam, The Public and Private Spheres*,
Social Research, Volume 70, No. 3, Fall 2003.

on me for financial support. The more negative response I received, the more persistent I became. I had decided to retain my right to practice law at all costs.

Sometimes I would pray that they would deny female lawyers the right to practice law, as they had done with female judges, so that my fate would be determined for me. But this did not happen. One day, I read an article written by a cleric named Sheikh Ali Tehrani, who claimed that *sharia* law did not prevent women from practicing law. By referring to a number of religious doctrines, Tehrani had proven that women were allowed to represent the cases of those who approached them. In fact, Tehrani claimed that according to religious law, everyone enjoyed the freedom to choose his legal representative, even if that representative was insane. Given the fact that people were free to employ "madmen" as their lawyers and advocates, surely a woman should not be denied the right to practice law, he concluded.

Therefore, based on Tehrani's interpretation, female lawyers were accorded a level of professional security. And so my prayers were not answered, and with the requests of those who had asked for me, an insane lawyer, to represent their cases, I had to continue going to the judiciary—a hellhole that truly burned my spirit.

The power of the attorney was gradually eroded by the encroaching and ever-expanding power of religious judges. It was as though the name of the street where the judiciary building was located, Davar—meaning judge or arbitrator—had become meaningless. In the years 1925-1932, the legal scholar Davar ended the unregulated reign of religious clerics in the court by calling for educated professionals to serve as judges. He also instituted a prosecutor in the court system, in an effort to defend the rights of the people and in line with modern legal systems. He insisted on professionalism and technical expertise within the court system. The penal code based on *sharia* law and religious punishments had dominated the legal system, but under the direction of Davar, it was replaced with modern law, which incorporated secular punishments. As a result of Davar's efforts, educated lawyers were allowed to become defenders of their clients' rights.

Within a few decades after the adoption of a new and modern legal system, the violent and inhumane punishments derived from *sharia* law, such as dismemberment of arms, fingers and legs, flogging, stoning, and the eye-for-an-eye concept of Qesas law, became non-existent. Relying on modern law and secular customs, the new judicial system approved the general penal code, which complemented the codes of conduct guiding criminal trials. Following this revolutionary transformation of the legal system, the bar association was founded and in time attained independence in 1955 (24 years before the Islamic Revolution).

By relying on the modernization policies of Reza Shah, Davar was able to strengthen the two wings of the Angel of Justice. These wings, which grew symbolically out of the body of a woman, were carved atop the judiciary building. The Angel of Justice is a blindfolded woman with tasseled hair and a sword in hand, designed by the judiciary as it arrived upon secular notions. Violent religious beliefs could not be tolerated by this angel and contradicted her nature. One of the wings represented the independent, educated and professional judge who relied on the law for making decisions, and the other wing represented the educated, professional lawyer who depended on the law. But despite the changes in the legal structure of the country, family disputes remained within the scope of power of the religious establishment and were based on *sharia* law. Clerics had the power to decide on all family disputes, such as marriage, divorce, custody and inheritance and made rulings on these issues from their offices, or *mahzars*. These rulings carried legal weight. The adoption of the Family Protection Law under Mohammad Reza Shah resulted in the creation of family support courts, which limited the absolute power of the religious establishment over family-related matters. After the revolution, however, Iran's civil law, which was based on *sharia* law and was drafted in between 1931 and 1934, was readopted and family issues once again became the sole domain of the religious establishment.

I remember arriving one day at the judiciary building as I was reviewing the achievements of Davar. The building was modern. Inside, the accused and the lawyers defending them were hard at work. Despite this fact, I felt as if the spirit of Davar had vacated the building. The house remained but was occupied by others— by those who favored *sharia* judgment. I felt that the Iran of Davar had been appropriated, that the Angel of Justice had been forced to wear a *chador* and as a result had taken to damning us all.

On another occasion I witnessed a pickup truck carrying several camels in its bed, stopped in front of the judiciary building. As it turned out, an accused man had been sentenced to pay a *dieh*[2] (blood money) in camels, and until he paid his fine his case could not be closed. It was as if I was simultaneously witnessing two images of the legal system. The camels were reminiscent of customary punishments in Arabia 1,500 years ago, and the body of the Angel of Justice carved atop the judiciary building represented the legal system of Iran and the modern world in the 20th century.

I pushed back the canvas curtain and like a roach, wearing all black, I entered the building, which was now called the Islamic Judiciary Building. One of the wings of the angle of justice had been burned. The other wing had been injured. When the board of directors of the Iranian bar association in 1979 refused to abide by the orders of the judiciary heads, Ayatollah Beheshti, who was at the time in charge of confiscation of property at the new judiciary, ordered the bar association to vacate its offices, located in the main building of the judiciary.

The bar association was forced to abide by this order and moved its offices to Saadi Avenue. After a short period, the members of the board of directors of the Iranian bar association were arrested. The female lawyer Ms. Batool Keyhani, the secretary of the board of directors, was sentenced to prison, charged with refusing to cooperate with the judiciary in vacating its offices. She spent two years in the women's section of Qasr prison, where she served her time with women arrested on charges of political crimes and prostitution. As a result, the Iranian bar association was transformed into a government entity, with a government employee appointed as its head. The government head rarely appeared at his post at the bar association, and it was rumored that he was appointed to 22 government posts and positions simultaneously.

---

[2] According to Article 294 of the Islamic Penal Code, *dieh* is paid as compensation for causing physical injury due to a criminal or negligent act. The compensation is paid to the person suffering the injury or, in the case of death, to those with rights to the blood of the injured, which includes blood relatives such as fathers, mothers, siblings or children.

In the absence of the appointed director, the custodian of the building who had worked in that post for some time took charge of the affairs of the bar association. The custodian had grown a full beard, and bruises caused by prayer stones, a testament to his pious nature and long hours spent at prayer, were visible on his forehead. Before the revolution, this custodian was always ready to serve the lawyers who came to the bar association, and he often demonstrated his respect by bowing in front of them. Now he was providing the judiciary officials with reports on the activities of the members of the bar association. In one report, he had claimed that Ms. Batool Keyhani, the secretary of the board of directors of the bar association, was surely guilty of a crime, as before the revolution she appeared at work with stylish and expensive boots.

It was a sad state. The uneducated custodian, who had initially been hired to serve tea and clean the building, now bearded with worry beads in hand, was providing incriminating reports about the members of the bar association to the judiciary heads, who often consulted with the custodian and relied on his reports to build false cases against the members of the bar. When I went to the bar association office to renew my license to practice law, I witnessed first hand that the custodian had taken charge of the affairs at the office, the lawyers had become inconsequential and the ever-absent government-appointed head of the bar was no where to be found, but was quickly eroding and destroying all of Davar's achievements for which he had worked for so long.

It was as if Iranian lawyers had instantly become orphaned. They avoided the offices of the bar association as much as they possibly could. And when they were forced to go the offices to purchase forms or to renew licenses, they found no sign of its independence, and no recourse for their complaints against the new judges and officials within the judiciary who treated them disrespectfully. These orphaned lawyers gradually demonstrated their state of discontent and disillusionment on the outside as a result, as their physical appearance—including their dress—began to worsen. Many closed their offices and many continued with their work, but suffered immensely as a result. And some joined the judiciary heads and the new judges and conspired with them to justify the actions of the state, and often to deny in the most inhumane manner the civil rights of Iranians in the name of Islam.

4

The Tehran judiciary was not very welcoming toward me. Whichever court I appeared in I returned empty handed. The language of the law had changed, and religious jurisprudence had replaced it. I was desperately unfamiliar with the religious terminology used by the cleric judges. I didn't know how I could overcome all the many obstacles I faced in my effort to practice law. Several months passed before a brilliant idea dawned upon me. I went to the bar association and wrote a letter. Along with the letter, I included a bribe and handed them both to the custodian at the bar association, who had now started running the place. He laughed a devilish laugh. He was pleased to see the lawyers in such a terrible state. He placed a number on the letter and told me not to worry, that he would take care of everything immediately.

In this letter, I had asked the bar association to introduce me as a public attorney for the First Criminal Court of Tehran. The first criminal courts tried cases with heavy and often violent religious punishments. The constitution of the Islamic Republic had stipulated that those facing criminal charges must be represented in court by an attorney, otherwise the validity of the court's decision would be in question. Those who could not afford an attorney would have one appointed for them. These attorneys were expected to provide their services on a pro-bono basis.

By relying on this law, I started the process of becoming a public attorney. With this strategy, I would be able to kill two birds with one stone. This position would allow me to develop better relations with the cleric judges and also, by representing clients on a pro-bono basis, I would be afforded the opportunity learn the new language of the law and new defense strategies within the Islamic legal system. This scheme was indeed very helpful in my efforts to continue practicing law.

I was invited on a regular basis to represent indigent clients. Each of these invitations was like a golden key, opening up the closed doors of the judiciary for me. The fear that I had felt toward the Islamic judiciary was now replaced with a sense of excitement about my opportunity to learn and enter the area of Islamic law. The judges, too, were very receptive. The minute they found out that I was a public defender, working for free, they felt reassured that I was not intent on encroaching upon their domain, nor was I out to "rob" my clients. They would invite me to sit and would offer me tea. They even provided me with the case files of my clients.

I would, in accordance with my responsibility, review and study the files to develop my understanding of the legal terminology. The judges and officials at the Judiciary were impressed with my commitment. They had never seen a public attorney work so seriously on behalf of her clients. They didn't realize that I was discovering the new area of law—their domain—in an effort to continue practicing law in my own country.

Every day, I would wear my manteau, an overcoat that women wore after the revolution as a form of *hejab* to cover themselves in accordance with Islamic law, and which was customary in professional settings, and I would put on my head scarf and pants, and with great excitement make my way to the courts. I would ride a street taxi and pay a double fare so that I could sit in the front seat by myself. My friends and neighbors imagined that I was making tons of money. Only I knew how and why I had chosen to take on this strange role. And the judges, impressed by my commitment to the cases I accepted, often working beyond the call of duty, would be considerate in their approach toward me. I was slowly gaining back the self-esteem I had lost.

I would listen intently to judges when they spoke of certain crimes and punishments, and to their suggestions for defense strategies and avenues for following legal cases. Upon leaving the court, I would write down all the new terminology, so that I could later find books that explained the Islamic jurisprudence and terms associated with my cases. I would search the bookstores for these books and slowly, in my library at home, my books on the constitutional revolution, poetry and the plays of Gholamhossein Saedi were replaced with new arrivals address-ing issues such as *hodood*[1] *qesas*[2] and *ta'zirat.*[3]

The often difficult judges who harbored anti-lawyer senti-ments, and who at the depths of their beings disapproved of fe-male lawyers, had become my instructors and teachers, guiding me through my professional learning and life so that I could be-

---

[1] *Hodood* is the plural form of the term *had,* which when roughly translated means limit or allotment. According to Article 13 of the Is-lamic Penal Code, punishments that have a preset limit are referred *to as hodood.* For example, the preset punishment for consumption of alcoholic beverages is 100 strikes of the whip. Accordingly, the judge cannot impose a punishment of flogging less than or greater than the *hodood* of punishment preset by the law.

[2] Article 14 of the Islamic Penal Code outlines the punishments, or *qe-sas,* intended for criminals accused and convicted of murder or physical assault. According to this article, the punishment inflicted upon the convicted criminal must be equal to the actual crime. In other words, *qesas* is the concept of "an eye for an eye," which had been brought into the legal framework. However, since citizens are accorded varying rights and weights of worth, including monetary value placed on the lives of individuals, in practice within the Islamic system, this law does not literally translate into "an eye for an eye." For example, if a Mus-lim man murders another Muslim man, he is labeled and treated as a murderer and must pay with his life. Yet if a Muslim man murders a Muslim woman, the murderer will be required to pay with his life only if the family of the murdered woman pays half of his blood money, since the blood price for a woman (the monetary value placed on her life) is half that of a man. The philosophy behind this practice is based on the unequal values placed on the lives of women and men within Islam. This philosophy directly contradicts international human rights standards, and has worked against women in Iran.

[3] *Ta'zirat is the plural of ta'zir.* Article 16 of the Islamic Penal Code outlines certain punishments that have not been fully defined according to *Sharia* law. In these cases the judge has leeway in deciding the type and degree of punishment, which can include imprisonment, fines and flogging. The amount of punishment varies according to the discretion of the judge, but must not exceed the limit (*Had*) defined by the law. For example, mingling between men and women who are not married is defined as a criminal act within the Islamic Penal System. A judge can therefore sentence those accused of this activity to the punishment of flogging. However, the number of strikes cannot exceed 74, accord-ing to the law for this crime.

come familiar with the new language of the revolution, the new culture and the new judicial system. The judges believed that I was a rich woman who was providing my services on a pro-bono basis out of the kindness of my heart. They didn't know that every month I would go straight to the Gold District on Karim Khan Zand Avenue to sell a prized possession—a gold bracelet, a few gold coins or a piece of jewelry—so that I would be able to meet my expenses. Yet in this game, I felt like the victor.

Some were confused by my strange behavior and believed that I had become a devout follower of Hezbollah. My strict observation of the *hejab* made my mother laugh. My daughter Lily would on occasion take out our family albums and examine pictures in which I was not wearing the *hejab*.

"Do you still have this blouse?" Lily would ask.

If I responded "yes," she would reply by saying, "Then leave it for me so that I can wear it when I grow up. You don't need these clothes anymore."

My husband had lost his soul in the radio speakers. He would spend all of his time listening to broadcasts of foreign radio programs, which would promise the end of the Islamic regime. Emotionally, he did not understand my situation. Only my mother understood how I felt and realized that I did not see this catastrophe as a short-lived event, and that I anticipated the survival of the Islamic regime. She understood that I wanted to test my own abilities in these new conditions, and at a minimum achieve what I had achieved before the revolution—recognition as a well-known writer and journalist, with an active social life. She understood that my life had at one unpredictable and cruel instant turned upside down. She understood that if it weren't for the revolution I would have achieved a respectable position in my professional life—that I would have become either a minister or a famous lawyer or a competent writer. My mother tried to console me and she approved of my strategy. What I did not understand at the time was that she was worried about me. My loneliness in this strange predicament pained her immensely. But her presence was a great source of support for me. I did not pay attention to the reaction of others, and instead continued along my own path of discovering the strange phenomenon that had surrounded me.

I had gradually become ugly. One day as I was passing by my mother, she complained, "Honey, you smell. Don't you change your clothes anymore?" My mother fully understood that I had only one Islamic manteau. It was as if I had made a pact with ugliness. I remember a retired judge, Mr. Nateghi, warning me on this issue as well. He was a judge I had known for some time and he always took pleasure in seeing me. He enjoyed my writings, which he read in the publications of the Shah's time, and every time we crossed paths he would discuss them with me. He made a point of encouraging me and giving me hope in my endeavors. I saw him one day around the judiciary building, where he had come to inquire about his retirement. He could not come to terms with the Islamic judicial system. Mr. Nateghi was a pleasant and handsome man, but on the day I saw him at the judiciary he looked morose and was frowning. Despite the fact that our glances had locked, it took him a little while to recognize me. Immediately, and in an extremely straightforward manner, he said, "Oh dear, how is it that you have become so ugly?"

I will never forget Nateghi's look of disdain at my full Islamic attire. I said goodbye quickly. I was upset by his reaction, but I consoled myself by admitting that each person's capacity is different. Some people don't have the capacity to coexist with ugliness, but I did, and as such, I would use this capacity to build something that would allow me to cope better with the destiny that had entrapped me. Ugliness was a precondition for surviving in that environment. I increased the pace of my steps, leaving behind me the past from which I had migrated. Where was I going? I did not know.

It seemed that I had gone to a land where women who had been sentenced to death by stoning for their indiscretions of love and lust would beg for my help. I had gone to a land where men with their backs wounded and infected due to flogging would send me messages from prison asking for my help. I had gone to a land where any pleasure-filled, social, primal and human act was an unforgivable sin. And on occasion, in this land, I would take up the case of a client accused of stealing who faced the possible dismemberment of his arm. I had gone to the depths of darkness and sometimes I felt like I was fully immersed in filth. As if I were drowning, I would raise my head for a bit, take a deep breath, and by doing so remain alive. In this land, I had the opportunity to become more familiar with the strange conditions of my life—a life in which I was a foreigner. In this strange place, the vast roots of thousands of years of tradition had risen from the depths of the murky earth to twist around me and tie my hands.

The government was not alone in this endeavor, to which I can attest. I had been witness on so many occasions to the requests of men begging the judge to sentence their cheating wives to death by stoning. I had seen rich victims solicit the judge to dismember the arms of the thief who had robbed them of their possessions. I witnessed fathers gratefully kiss the hands of judges who had ordered their sons to be flogged. They would explain to the judges, "Perhaps your punishment will tame my disobedient son." The truth was that these hidden traditions, with their tangled roots, were alive in each and every one of us. We would never have seen them, but with the revolution and an Islamic government as their excuse, these traditions reared their heads to take hostage the Angel of Justice.

But in this strange land where I had recently arrived, I did see the goddess of love. Repeatedly I witnessed her battling the judges of the Islamic Republic for the right to love. She would appear on the scene not from the towering heavens of mythology, but from the depths of poverty and backwardness, humming the melody of love. The judges of the Islamic Republic did not understand that this land was influenced as much by violent traditions as it was by the mythology of love. When faced with such realities, the judges would shiver in fear that Iran was indeed not the guarded land of the ruler with absolute power. This was no longer the tame land ruled by Sultans and Sheikhs, who were chosen by and represented God and who wielded uncontrolled and absolute power.

Judges passed down tens of flogging sentences daily for women who had refused to observe the *hejab* or who were unwilling to abide fully and appropriately. On each day, the judges faced yet another group of women accused of not observing the forced *hejab*, of mingling with men in private or public spaces, of laughing out loud, of drinking or of simply enjoying life. Despite the fact that the women would wipe their lips with tissue and wash off their eyeliner prior to appearing before the judges, their lips remained red from lipstick and the black of the eyeliner could still be seen below their eyes. After being sentenced, the women would receive their floggings and then inevitably return to normal life. The makeup bags, the changing style of manteaus, the liner beneath the eyes, the eyeshadow, the strands of colored hair that would seep out from under scarves, and the friendships and connections made at social gatherings were not forgotten with a few strikes of a painful, skin-tearing whip. Iranians had lived for many years with social freedoms and without fear, at least with respect to social activities. They weren't willing to surrender these freedoms, even under the threat of being flogged.

Through my clients' cases, such as those sentenced to stoning or accused of adultery and free sexual relations, I became intimately familiar with earthly passions offered by the goddess of love. Most of the indigent clients I represented on a pro bono basis came from religious families. Their commitment to love was reminiscent of mythological tales. Earthly sacrifices, meant to free their lover and partner in crime, included willingness to die. Often, they were more focused on freeing their lovers than they were on saving themselves. When asked to confess and seek absolution according to Islamic traditions, they would agree conditionally, asking for the release of their lovers in return— lovers to whom they were not married under Islamic law. In my eyes, Iran had turned into the land of lovers—of female lovers for whom tradition, Islamic *sharia*, the law and patriarchy had conspired to make love taboo. These women were willing to pay for love with their lives, and each and every one of them had appeared before me, swearing me to Fatemeh, the daughter of the prophet, begging me to defend them in such a way that would not only spare them their own lives, but would also ensure the freedom of their coconspirators in love.

5

By the force of a miracle and by becoming a public court-appointed pro bono attorney, I had managed to develop better relations with the clerical judges, and like a spider, I had become trapped by the web of the Islamic judicial system. The laws had twisted themselves around my hands and feet. The essence of these laws had become a tool for the cleric judges. Defense lawyers could use the laws as tools in their trade only if their interests were in line with those of the judges. Otherwise, they were helpless. The cleric judges, who had come to occupy the bench in place of secular judges, despite professing to abide by *sharia* law would dismiss all the protective measures incorporated within Islamic law, in an effort to make an easy and quick ruling. For example, many Islamic laws, especially in cases involving life or a person's good name, make it difficult to obtain the proof necessary to convict individuals. In cases of adultery, for example, *sharia* law calls for the adulterer to utter a confession of adultery four times. Each confession must be made in a different instant or occasion and must be voluntary, provided without either physical or emotional pressure, before it is valid and used as proof to convict the individual. On one occasion, a client of mine who had confessed to adultery was forced by the cleric judge to leave the courtroom and re-enter four times, each time confessing to adultery. With this, the judge ensured a speedy ruling.

The constitution allowed judges to assess their cases and hand down sentences based on credible *fatwas*[1]. As such, interpreta-

---

[1] Article 167 of the constitution of the Islamic Republic of Iran reads as follows: A judge is required to try to find out the sentence of every lawsuit in codified laws. If he fails to find out, he must issue a sentence on the matter under consideration based on authentic Islamic sources or authoritative religious injunctions [*fatwas*]. He cannot refrain from

tions of the law were so varied that in a system like this, a defense lawyer was rendered helpless. With the presence of court-appointed lawyers, however, the cases and court proceedings took on a legitimate form, and the unjust sentences passed down by these judges could not be contested based on the absence of legal representation. The public attorney had become a nail in the coffin of justice.

In an effort to change my role and redefine my work, I began to reduce the number of pro bono cases I took on and increased my other cases. With the passing of time, I came to believe more and more that something needed to be done. The eight-year war between Iran and Iraq in 1981 had increased political tensions. The Iranian public had become oppressed and tired, and people spent most of their time waiting in food and cigarette lines. Political activists who had opposed the regime were either in prison or in hiding, or had fled to foreign countries. They felt as if they had lost their will and their ideals to the clerics. There was no time, no energy and no capacity to ask questions or resist. Questions had defected from the political realm and had been relegated to the social realm. The Iranian public would use the time spent waiting in line for food to seek solace and complain to one another. People's faces had become cold and hopeless. No one was aware of or interested in knowing what took place in Iran's courts.

Police patrols would cruise the streets of Tehran picking up and arresting women who had failed to properly observe the *hejab*, and take them to prison. At night, committees of morality police would set up roadblocks and stop cars to search their passengers and their interiors. These committees were usually manned by teenagers. As the number of committees increased, public harassment amplified and the latent objection to the situation took on new and varying forms. The dark atmosphere of the city shed light on the revolt of women who would take on the morality policy in physical one-on-one fights. In the absence of

---

dealing with the suit and issuing a judgment on the pretext of silence, inadequacy, abridgement or contradiction to codified laws.

The problem is that the constitution does not stipulate which *fatwa*s are credible and which are not, and allows judges great leeway in deciding which *fatwa*s to follow in their rulings. As a result, the *fatwa* can be in direct and sharp contradiction to human rights standards.

alcoholic drinks and bars, bootleg liquor was produced in high quantities within homes.

Tulips brightened the city's neighborhood while attesting to the martyrdom of young men. The last will and testament of these young martyrs was reproduced and distributed broadly. In their last will and testament, they called upon women to remain pure, virtuous and committed to Islam by observing Islamic dress and maintaining strict *hejab*. Posters, banners and murals would consistently remind women of their duty to respect the sacrifice of martyrs in defense of the state and religion by retaining strict Islamic dress. The words of martyrs were all somehow related to the *hejab* of women, and the *hejab* had become forever linked to the blood of the martyrs.

Now entering the building of the judiciary required not only that women wear a manteau or over coat, slacks, a head covering and black socks and shoes, but at times access to certain offices and floors of the judiciary where the clerics gathered was contingent upon the recitation of a secret password. The prosecutor's office, which was located near the Golestan Palace and the Ark Mosque, was one of those places where a secret password was required for entry. These passwords would change regularly in honor of the latest battles on the war front, in which Iranian soldiers were engaged in combat with Iraq.

One day when I entered the building with my client Zahra H., to see the prosecutor in an effort to discuss her case with him, the secret password was "Ya Zahra." Upon entering the building I got a small scrap of paper from the woman at the door. The secret password was scribbled on this paper in sloppy handwriting. I used the secret password, as one would use a passport upon entering a foreign land, to enter the office of the prosecutor. Zahra, her two children and I entered the office. We wanted to let him know of the difficult predicament of Zahra's children so that perhaps he could provide us with some assistance. We were told that the prosecutor had left for prayers, so we waited, but he did not return. Finally, we were told that the prosecutor had gone to the Ark Mosque to take part in the funeral of a number of martyrs who had been killed at the hands of the Mojahedin Khalgh[2], opposed to the Islamic Republic.

---

[2] Mojahedin Khalgh Organization (MKO) is an armed resistance group with Islamic-Marxist ideology. The group resisted the Shah's regime

Finally when the prosecutor returned, without even hearing her case, he told Zahra: "Tell that roughneck who has stuck you with these kids to come and collect them." Zahra explained that her husband, Hamid, was an Afghani and did not have legal papers. Their marriage was in accordance with Islamic traditions, but she did not have any documents to prove that she was married. She explained that they had been unable to obtain the necessary documents form the Ministry of the Interior to register their marriage. Zahra continued to tell her story to the prosecutor and in doing so explained the many difficulties facing Iranian women married to Afghans. She said that because they could not register their marriages, they were unable to get birth certificates for their children. As a result, the children were not allowed to attend school.

After hearing what Zahra had to say, the prosecutor replied curtly. "I already told you. Give these children to their Afghan father so that they can leave the country and you can save yourself."

"I am Iranian," Zahra explained. "Why can't I get a birth certificate for my children?"

"You shouldn't have married an Afghan national," the prosecutor replied. "Iranian women married to foreigners can't pass on their nationality to the children born of these marriages. These are divine laws. You can't fight the laws of God."

At this point, I opened my mouth to add to what Zahra had said. The phone rang. The prosecutor dismissed us and without any further explanation he said, "So long." We hadn't left the office yet when the prosecutor called me to his desk. "Are you crazy to accept these types of cases?" he asked. "Aren't there any better clients you can take on?" I didn't have the patience to respond to him, so I left. Zahra and her two hungry, undocumented children, who could in reality have been labeled as illegitimate, bid me farewell so they could go back to Afsarieh, in southern Tehran, where they lived. Zahra H. and her two innocent children were alone in their dilemma and the law could not help.

---

through armed conflict within Iran and joined efforts to bring about the revolution. The Mojahedin Khalgh, after the establishment of the Islamic Republic, began another armed resistance effort in Iran and eventually continued its resistance abroad.

On my way home, I began to think again that there must be something I could do to expose the law and its shortcomings for the Iranian people. It seemed that exposing the limited capacity of Islamic laws, in a language that would not be labeled as blasphemous or anti-Islamic, was imperative. It was difficult, however, to begin such a discussion during wartime. The judicial system, because of the presence of clerics, seemed to be turning into a fortress where all points of entry for human rights standards were closed. Criticizing the current situation seemed impossible. The press was under tight control. The state-run television and radio broadcasting system was the mouthpiece for the government and was charged with justifying the current situation. The Iranian public could be likened to ants spending their whole day gathering enough food for their subsistence. At night they would take refuge in their own homes, pull the thick shades, and rest a bit.

Our house had become the place for the exchange of experiences within the Islamic Republic. My little daughter Lily would bring home stories from school. These stories were new for us. She would tell us how she was interrogated all day by her religious teacher about the goings on in our house. My husband would bring home tales of his experiences in the long food and cigarette lines, sprinkled with bits of news he had heard from foreign language broadcasts. My mother would recount her encounters with the newly pious neighbors. But my experiences were so bitter indeed that, every time I retold them, they would disrupt the members of my household. Stories of floggings and stoning; stories of forgiveness and guilt. These could not be recounted. I would hide them away, in the corners of my soul, so that I could read fairy tales to my small child instead.

One night, my mother tore up the book I had bought my daughter. The book was about a little poor girl who had to sell matches to make a living. My mother claimed that when we were all suffering so much and were so depressed at the state of affairs of our society, we should not burden small children with stories about poverty and loneliness. My mother had come to the conclusion that amidst the storm we needed to appreciate the little bit of shelter that we managed to find. She believed that we should be content with our little bits of happiness. So after that, I would appear daily in an arena that had been colored by blood, and war, and murder, and stoning, and at night I put all those adventures aside and read happy childhood fairytales for my girl. Eventually story time became an escape for both Lily and me. I would ride the golden wings of fairytales, picking stars from the skies along with Lily, and I would distance myself from the filth of what had become my daily reality.

One of the pro bono cases I took on was that of a woman accused of murder. When the case was over, I went to one of the districts of the criminal court, presided over by Judge Shekar. During that visit, I happened to overhear a conversation in which Shekar was confiding in his friends, who had come to visit him. Shekar was a young and religious judge. Some claimed that he was a seminary student, studying to be a cleric. Based on my previous interactions with him, I realized that he was not looking for wealth and was not willing to take bribes in relation to his cases. For years, this court over which he presided would oversee cases having to do with the interests of the Islamic Republic. The duration of the cases were usually short, and death and *qesas* sentences passed by the court were carried out quickly. Without fear, this judge would with great ease hand out death and *qesas* sentences. He had come to be admired by the judiciary officials, while instilling fear in the hearts of the public.

Special cases were usually referred to Shekar's court. Such cases included those needing to be addressed urgently, and usually carried violent sentences intending to create fear and quell possibilities of revolt. Many who appeared before Judge Shekar were from poor neighborhoods, where the possibility of revolt was always strongest. Shekar. These urgent cases, as defined by the Islamic Republic, were in need of a speedy response. For example, Mr. Shekar was once called to court during the New Year's celebrations so that he could, based on his religious beliefs, hand down a sentence that called for pushing a group of men off a cliff. These men had been accused of raping some boys. Mr. Shekar relied on his understanding of *sharia* law and would often rely on the interpretations of *sharia* from the *mojtahed* he followed, to determine swift and often cruel punishments for those he viewed as criminals. He did not falter in these decisions and his sentences were always the most extreme.

Perhaps that day, in his office, was a special day in the life of Mr. Shekar, who had sentenced so many people to death. On that day, I witnessed Mr. Shekar speaking to his friends about his nightmares. He told his friends that he had grown tired and so had gone to see Ayatollah Yazdi, who at the time headed the judiciary, to ask for a change in assignment. He explained his reason for this request. It seemed that Shekar, a small-framed judge, in whose being religious fervor and belief had forever fused itself with blood, had begun to have nightmares in which he was being executed. To Shekar's request Ayatollah Yazdi had replied negatively, stating that it was not a good idea to transfer him to another post.

At the outset, when you first took on this position, your hands would shiver every time you wanted to sign off on a sentence of *qesas*. But this is no longer the case. If we bring a new judge to preside over this district court to oversee our 'special cases,' he will not be able to address the cases with the same power and precision that you have learned to do. He will not be able to sentence criminals to *qesas* as easily. The Islamic Republic needs you.

Mr. Shekar's friends praised Ayatollah Yazdi for recognizing the important role that the young judge played in the district court. We left Mr. Shekar alone in his courtroom, which could be more appropriately described as a slaughterhouse. The tea they served me that day tasted like blood, and for hours after leaving the court its taste remained with me.

Slowly, I came to understand that the Arabic word *dam* meant blood in discussions of Islamic jurisprudence. This term was related to murder and other criminal offenses to which a value would be assigned. The owners of blood had different values placed on their rights. In other words the term *life,* which was defined by the word *dam,* had many dimensions to it and a number of different values. There is an Iranian saying that claims, "No one man's blood is more colorful than another's." In human rights terms this means that all humans are valued equally, they have equal rights, and the rights of one should not be valued over the rights of the other. But in Islamic jurisprudence this definition was not acceptable.

In the Islamic judicial system, the life of a man is more valuable than the life of a woman and the blood money (*dieh*) assigned to a woman is half that of a man's. The blood of a non-Muslim who is murdered at the hands of a Muslim is not very colorful, it seems. The blood money paid for the murder of a non-Muslim, such as a Christian, Jew or Zoroastrian, is not nearly as much as the blood money paid for the murder of a Muslim. In the year 2004, 25 years after the revolution, because of international pressures, this law was changed. But the under the Islamic law, the lives of non-Muslims who are members of religions not recognized by the Islamic Republic, such as Bahais or Buddhists, are given no value. These people are classified under Islamic law as *mahdur ol-dam,* meaning that under *sharia* law their lives hold no value. And as interpreted by the law, if a Muslim intentionally murders someone who is classified as *mahdur ol-dam,* he faces no punishment. The murder of a Muslim person who has disavowed Islam, or a person who has insulted the leaders of the Islamic Republic, is allowed and is not punishable under Islamic law.

This Islamic term was turned into a winning card that was then used by the Islamic Republic to rob those deemed to oppose the regime of life. This Islamic term was in fact broadened by the regime and by cleric judges and entered into the judicial system, in an effort to fight freely those they believed to belong to opposition groups. Thinkers such as Mohammad Mokhtari, Mohammad Jafar Pooyandeh, and Parvaneh and Darioush Forouhar were murdered. And this law was used as the justifying basis for the actions of the murderers.

In another case, I represented the family of a Jewish woman who had been intentionally murdered by a Muslim man. I was able to prove the guilt of the accused man during the trial. However, the happiness I felt from winning the case was quickly replaced by the sadness and frustration that overwhelmed me when I read the sentence issued by the judge. The man was ordered by the court to pay 25,000 tomans as blood money to the family of the woman who was murdered. The fact that she was Jewish was taken into consideration, as was the fact that she was a woman. In the end, the sentence called for payment of blood money, which was half of what would have to be paid for the murder of a Jewish man.

It was as if the world had crashed around me. I hurried home. I took my daughter Lily into my arms. She had just returned from school, where she had been given a plastic piggy bank in the shape of the Qods building. She explained that they had given her the piggy bank so that she could collect money to help the war effort, which was touted as a sacred fight in defense of state and religion. There was a little note on the piggy bank:

"The road to Jerusalem passes through Karbala[3]"

In one day, Lily and I had experienced first hand the Islamic Republic's views of the followers of other religions. Lily, who was 6 years old, was happy that with her help toward the war effort, she could assist in ending the occupation of Jerusalem, and I, a 36-year-old defense attorney, was sick to my stomach at the fact that a Muslim murderer had been able to kill a Jewish woman, without fear of any real reprisal.

Lily and I, distracted by our own thoughts and experiences, held each other until we fell asleep. She slept thinking of the lofty dreams of the Islamic Republic, and I slept thinking of the nightmare of the judicial system within the Islamic Republic of Iran.

---

[3] The government defined the war with Iraq as a holy war in defense of state and religion. This slogan was intended to excite young people into joining the war effort. Jerusalem as the ultimate destination for Muslims seeking to right injustices was promoted as an ideal for those wishing to sacrifice their lives in the name of religion and God. Karbala was symbolically the battle that must be won before achieving victory in Jerusalem.

6

I did not dare enter the political scene with the intention of exposing the corruption of the judiciary and the shortcomings of the law to which I was a daily witness. My introduction to Shahla Lahiji, who later became the first female Iranian publisher, strengthened in both of us the notion of taking up a historical research project. The project examined the mythology and mythological beliefs about women in the greater Persian culture of which the current Iran is only a small portion. Se we set out to examine the historical status and significance of women in this area of the world.

The first book on the subject, titled *The Identity of Iranian Women*, was published in 1992 by Roshangaran Publishing, Shahla Lahiji's publishing house[1], which was founded at about the same time. We both worked consistently for two years to conduct the research for this book. The end result of our research allowed us to put forth the proposition that women enjoyed high positions and great respect within Persian culture and society. In fact, their status was impacted negatively with the emergence of monotheistic religions. But, during a time when multiple gods were worshiped and before the discovery of writing, women enjoyed high positions and great respect within Persian society.

Our historical findings demonstrated that prior to the entrance of Arians to Iran and the division of the land between a number of tribes, the people of Persia, like those of neighboring countries, were ruled by a matriarchal system and worshiped, like many others in the region, the mother goddess.[2]

---

[1] Lahiji, Shahla and Kar, Mehrangiz, *The Identity of Iranian Women,* translated from Persian, Roshangaran Publishing, Tehran, Iran, 1992. Page 81.
[2] Ibid., 78.

The oldest documented incident attesting to the power of women in the land and culture of Persia was traced back to 6000 B.C., or approximately 8,000 years ago. Persia includes the area of land which falls between the Caspian Sea to the north, and the Persian Gulf to the south. The Zagros Mountains divided the western region of this land into western and eastern sections; the modern geographical area is attached to the central desert.[3]

In other words, Persia not only encompassed the current borders of Iran, but included the lands of Iran's neighbors. These geographical areas not only shared their common allegiance to the Persian Empire, but also shared many common cultural practices and beliefs. The Persian Empire included old civilizations, which in the prehistoric eras experienced the transition from hunting societies to agrarian societies. The examples of women's power in these societies are plentiful, including their initiative and role in leading wars and battles.[4]

Thousands of years before tribal groups migrated to this land, the people of Persia who made this land their home enjoyed a rich civilization. This civilization viewed women as superior and accorded women the power and authority that was indicative of and common within agrarian societies. As such, it is a misnomer to limit the richness of the Persian civilization to the period following the migration of the Aryans, as the culture and civilization of the people of this land was indeed rich before this historic event.

Researchers and historians have explained and documented the presence of women in positions of power during the transition to agrarian culture for the area identified as the Persian Empire. The worship of the mother goddess is one of the oldest documented religious practices in the history of mankind—a practice which took root in the early periods of civilization. This religion predates the worship of multiple gods and the emergence of monotheistic practices, which tend to be modeled after patriarchal practices that view the father figures and male as the ultimate authorities and as sacred. With the transition to agrarian life, the role of the mother goddess as the symbol of birth and reproduction of life became clearer. The mother goddess soon became the symbol of nature's protection and the symbol of life

---

[3] Ibid., 60.
[4] Ibid., 83.

and birth. The mother goddess also became the protector of mankind during death and life after death. The mother goddess became the protector of humans and was worshiped for responding to the totality of their needs and demands.

Likewise the researchers have found that during a period dating back about 10,000 years B.C. it has been reported that the Persian Empire and the region surrounding it experienced certain significant advances. Human beings who previously relied on heavy weapons as tools for hunting were successful in building lightweight tools made of bones. This period also marks the start of the production of clay and ceramic earthenware. Both of these developments were significant achievements allowing for advances in the state of life of human beings.

The production of light weight tools and ceramic ware are believed to have been carried out by women. Historical discoveries have proven that in this region in fact it was women who produced clay pots and dishes.

In general, in the old Persian civilization women enjoyed an elevated level of status and power. For example, women were charged with the important task of keeping lit the flames of fires, which provided support and protection and contributed to the sustenance of communal life. Women's talents, power and intelligence in carrying out the duties they were accorded allowed them to raise their status and eventually even surpass the status and position of men within these communities.

The elevation of women's status was so great indeed that it led to the emergence of matriarchal systems. Women's particular roles within the community, as mothers and the protectors of children and the family unit, transformed them into heavenly beings. Women became the symbol of life and creation and the mother goddess was fashioned in the image of women.

The position of women within the Persian culture was so revered and respected indeed that when the Aryans entered this region, they too accepted this interpretation of women's superior status and incorporated its related practices into their own traditions.

7

The findings of my research on women allowed me to become more sensitive to the repression of women and their diminished status within modern society. Much of the power usurped from women was done in the name of Islam in the last half of the 20th century. But the political atmosphere of the country and the eight-year war between Iran and Iraq did not leave an opportunity for addressing the question of women's status or objecting to the treatment of women. Likewise, the time for carrying out efforts designed to raise sensitivities among the Iranian public about women's issues and needs was not appropriate.

My professional life was faced with the contradictions that resulted from the corruption I witnessed on a daily basis within the judiciary system. The violent laws that had become the tools of my trade continued their domination in this very difficult period. My private life and our household environment had become over-politicized and a sense of bitterness could be felt within. Along with Shahla Lahiji, I had been able to complete a research project and publish a book about the last millennium, but I was unable to write about and publish what I witnessed and experienced on a daily basis within the court system. Censorship was rampant and the Islamic Republic was fast at work in its efforts to carry out bloody crackdowns against political and revolutionary groups that were trying to influence the development and the shape of the new government. Freedom of speech was indeed nonexistent.

My consistent presence in the judicial scene impacted my life negatively and stole any hope for happiness derived from the smaller pleasures of life. In the mornings I would go to an area of Tehran where the loudspeakers at the Ark Mosque, connected to the Judiciary Building, would blast requiems mourning the death of martyrs who had lost their lives in defense of Islam and the nation in the war with Iraq. In this part of the city justice, in contrary to our initial expectation of the revolution, was unattainable.

In the afternoons, the same people who were searching for and had found no sign of the Angel of Justice in the judiciary of the Islamic Republic would pour into the offices of their lawyers, so that perhaps they could finally find a solution to their problems. It seemed that the Angel of Justice had vacated these offices as well. Lawyers did not know how to respond to the needs of their clients. Some judges expected bribes for those cases infected with the stench of blood and money, which were deemed also to be sensitive. Without these bribes, lawyers could not expect a ruling in their favor. In the political cases, however, the lawyers had no influence or power whatsoever.

Every so often, the afternoon papers would run headlines that brought to the public news of the execution of those suspected of political activities against the state. These headlines or news pieces would usually read as follows: "A number of anti-revolutionaries, spies, *mohareb* and *mofsed-e filarz* (regime opponents/combatants or promoters of corruption)[1] were executed today." That was all that was mentioned and nothing else!

The Iranian people quickly understood that they could not fight the injustice that surrounded them. Each person chose his

---

[1] *Mohareb* and *mofsed-e filarz* are those accused of taking effective action to overthrow the Islamic Republic. According to the law, there is no definition for political opposition or political crimes. Rather this type of opposition in the law is defined as an opposition to God and religion, via opposition to the "Islamic State." For this reason, those accused of political crimes are treated very harshly and receive the highest, most violent of punishments. These punishments include execution by firing squad, hanging, dismemberment of the right arm, dismemberment of the left leg, and exile. The judge has the right to choose the type of punishment for these crimes. The penal codes related to these crimes demonstrate that in the Islamic Republic, political crimes and political criminals are not officially recognized, but are seen as combating God and promoting corruption on earth. As a result, the government and the judicial system do not require themselves to adhere to and observe the rights of those accused of political crimes, and respond with great violence.

Articles 183-188, 190-196 and 504 of the Islamic Penal Code of Iran outline these crimes and their related punishments.

own strategy for life – one that allowed him to live and to carry on. I used my feminine nature, and in an effort to resist that which was beyond my capacity to withstand, I chose pregnancy and birth. On the verge of menopause, when pregnancy becomes a difficult and arduous task, as I approached the age of 41, I gave birth to a little girl. Born on January 8, 1985, we named her Azadeh. I spent the entire nine months of my pregnancy loitering around the Judiciary Building. I forced the judges to tolerate my female presence – the very same judges who had, through a conspiracy of coincidence and fate, appeared at an astonishing point in history, at a time and place that was forever marked with blood, tears and corruption.

When Azadeh was born healthy, I came to question all the scientific and medical findings that suggested the health of the unborn child was intrinsically tied to the pregnant mother's ability to take care of herself, and to maintain a state of psychological calm during her pregnancy. I spent all my days of pregnancy, except the very last few, in the tension-ridden environment of the Judiciary Building. There was no sign of calm or relaxation in that environment. The sirens warning of possible bombings added to the sense of stress and chaos that existed in the judiciary. I felt as if the little girl that was growing in my womb had given me her blessing. She accepted my presence in this strange place and would somehow allow me to move forward in accordance with my fate. Everyone believed that I was carrying a boy. But I, a woman who was growing old, who was daily wearing down under the pressure and stress of her life, felt differently. Only a girl could alleviate the sense of distress that encompassed my life, by adding to it some balance and consistency.

At night when I returned home from my office, just a look from my two daughters, Lily and Azadeh, who were 10 years apart in age, was enough to help me in regaining my strength. My unexpected and late pregnancy had added to my physical and emotional strength. I was preparing to take on the task of documenting some of the extraordinary historical developments in the country of my birth in which I had chosen to live. I had lost my mother at this point and could only depend on myself to carry out my responsibilities as a mother to two growing girls. The strength that I derived from my role as a mother was so great that

I drew upon it as a measure to ensure my active presence and involvement in the developments around me.

My husband, Siamak Pourzand, committed his time and energy to caring for our newborn daughter, Azadeh. The developments of 1979 had disoriented my husband, who loved and respected the Shah. He knew that this new government would not tolerate his presence. At the time of the revolution, he worked as part of the Public Relations Team at the Ministry of Education. After the revolution, by relying on a newly passed law, he chose to retire from his post at the Ministry of Education. The law allowed for the early retirement of government employees with 20 years of employment history. With this new law, Siamak was able to volunteer for early retirement, but staying at home for him was an arduous and torturous task and was difficult for the rest of us to witness as well. Siamak wished for and followed closely the political developments that promised to bring down the Islamic Republic. He waited for a day when he could once again become active and take his place within Iran's press and media community.

One winter night in 1986, officers from the Revolutionary Courts of the Islamic Republic entered our house and took Siamak with them. His arrest, given the fact that he had refrained from public activity since the beginning of the revolution, was very much unexpected for us. That night, a mask of sadness overtook the faces of our two daughters, which to this day has never faded.

They released Siamak after two months. He was a broken man, with a stench of not having bathed, sporting a long beard. During the time of his imprisonment they had denied him the right to bathe. He was not even allowed to get a haircut. To this day, even Siamak has no clue why he was arrested; nor why he was released.

When I went to Evin Prison to present them with a deed of property, which was to serve as Siamak's bail, a precondition to his release, I happened—purely by accident and despite being blindfolded—to catch a glimpse of the cover of his case file. The file read: "Charge: Monarchist."

So, this was how our small family got acquainted with prison, solitary confinement and torture. Our children quickly learned that danger was always lurking close by. I understood that the issue at hand was not so simple and that this situation would not go away with the arrest and imprisonment of my husband – someone with no political affiliations, and no history of political activism. They had arrested him based on information obtained from a wiretap on our phone and through the scrutiny of his ideas and beliefs. I realized that this ordeal would in all likelihood be repeated.

Our friends encouraged Siamak to wait until the travel restrictions placed on him came to an end and then leave the country. They encouraged him to join his friends and colleagues who had been active in the media and the press during the Shah's time and who were now active within foreign language broadcasts outside Iran. They comprised some of the groups opposed to the Islamic Republic. Siamak did not heed their advice and chose instead a life restricted to the realm of his home, a private rather than public life, and by so doing he chose to stay in Iran rather than leave for another country.

8

We have approached the dusk of another day. The political atmosphere of the country does not leave legal defenders satisfied. This restrictive environment of the Iranian judiciary makes the defense lawyers feel as if they are playing the role of a cadaver—wholly unable to have any impact.

As I sit in my office, the doorbell rings. A young Irish woman with a handsome face who is carrying a bunch of flowers enters. . In fear of the forced Islamic dress codes in Iran, she has covered herself in a form of *hejab* so extreme that she looks ridiculous. Smiling, she introduces herself:

"I'm Liz Doset, a reporter with the BBC."

Confused, I look at her. "What can I do for you?" I asked.

She places her press identification in the palm of my hand and says: "You are one the people whom I was interested in visiting with while in Iran."

I sit with her. We begin a discussion on women's rights within the family. The reporter asks me to explain to her the laws that govern divorce. She asks permission to record this short interview. I am tired and eager to find an outlet for discussing the difficulties facing women in Iran, so I provide a short explanation in my broken English, which she records. Liz Doset leaves my office a victor.

The war had been over for some time. We could feel the presence of foreign reporters in the country. The Iranian government had been giving them visas, and they mostly stayed in hotels under the control of Information Ministry officers. The intellectuals and leading experts were still hesitant to speak with foreign reporters. Everyone was scared. But the reporters were persistent. They understood that state-sanctioned censorship was extreme, and that Iranians felt forced into silence. The foreign reporters understood that those alienated by this system would be willing to break their silence and talk. It would only take a little coaxing. Though they also understood that these people would have to take care.

The foreign reporters quickly learned how to maneuver the complicated laws and regulations of the Islamic Republic. They also discovered quickly the increasing level of corruption that existed in Iranian society, where your money could easily facilitate any connection. They learned quickly how to identify those officials, however few in number, at the Ministry of Culture and Islamic Guidance who would be willing to help them—officials who within their agency were strictly controlled by the more extremist groups in the Iranian political scene.

It seemed that Liz Doset had learned all the intricate workings of the system of the Islamic Republic. She was staying at the Laleh Hotel, formerly the Intercontinental, on Fatemi Avenue. She explained that her fear did not allow her to sleep at night. Her hotel was directly across the street from my law offices. My interview with Liz Doset was the start of an eventful period in my life. On that evening when she entered my office, I was not able to fully anticipate the consequences of her visit and our interview. That night I did not sleep. I kept visualizing the colonial games of the British and wondered if my interview with Liz Doset may have been a mistake. Also, I was worried about the Iranian security forces and wondered if I had finally given them the excuse they were looking for.

I overcame my fear in the days that followed. I decided I had the right to use the international media to discuss the legal and judicial shortcomings of the Iranian system, especially if all other options for voicing a differing opinion were closed within Iran. On the other hand, I had grown accustomed to the fear that followed my interview with Liz Doset. With every minute that passed, I came to realize that I had broken down another barrier and in so doing I was able to distance myself from the swamp that had overtaken and was destroying my professional life.

The happiness that I felt as a result of having connected with international media outlets played a great role in alleviating my fear even further. Of course, I should explain that I was fully aware of my own situation, and provided the international media with interviews in a manner so as not to create undue sensitivity within the security forces of the government. I did not intend to create a situation in which I would no longer be able to continue my work. For years, I was like a calm river, spilling into the foundation of the international media sources.

The foreign journalists, who had finally found their way to Iran after the end of the eight-year war with Iraq, rarely found anyone willing to risk his safety enough to talk with them. So, the few of us who were willing to take such risks and to talk to reporters were hounded. The reporters had been able to take the words and ideas of people from inside a country where people were too frightened by the prospects of prison, torture and execution to speak, for the world to hear. This was a country whose revolution was almost a decade old, and which had been virtually closed to the outside world for the duration of that time.

While our fear was obvious to those outside the country, those who risked their safety and well-being by giving interviews too were fully cognizant of the need to keep themselves safe, and out of the bloody hands of the intelligence forces. In a strange twist of fate, from inside a house that had long become accustomed to stories about solitary confinement, torture and illegal trials, issues surrounding women's rights in Iran were broadcast through the radio waves for the whole world to hear. Through this development, the voice of the Iranian woman was broadcast by the Persian language radio programs to foreign countries. This voice was calm and careful in analyzing and criticizing the laws that governed women and children in the Islamic Republic.

On occasion I would hear reactions to my words and opinions, broadcasted by these radio programs, on the streets of Tehran. I came to believe that even in a silence that was as heavy as death, one had the ability to speak and express objection, and the people of the world would listen. I had come to realize how constructive the old Persian saying, "Nothing is unattainable," actually was.

An aggressive government monthly by the name of *Sobh* (Morning) and a special daily that was published for the purpose of promoting the state's propaganda outside of Iran, *Keyhan Havaii* (Keyhan Air), tried to silence me by printing accusatory and inflammatory articles about me. They were clearly frightened by the strategy I had chosen in an effort to expose the inhumane laws of the Islamic Republic. My calm demeanor, which lacked any sign of excitement that comes from hate or disrespect, was dangerous for them. The articles published against me in these publications were intended to raise the sensitivities of the security forces with respect to my activities. They didn't realize that their insults actually gave me self-confidence. Additionally, these insults and their focus on me forced me to perfect my strategy, without actually undermining my message. My words were not bitter, but my objections and my criticisms were expressed loudly and clearly. My words were crafted in such a manner as to make clear that I did not intend to overthrow the regime, and my analysis and criticisms were such that Islam and the Muslims were never ridiculed, humiliated or offended.

Other experts and activists who chose to join our small numbers and engage in interviews with the foreign press applied the same strategies in expressing their objections. After a few years, these people, without even realizing it or intending it and without an effort toward organizing a resistance, created a powerful front and would regularly talk with foreign broadcasts. Without even agreeing with each other on issues, these people became major players within the Iranian scene as critics, and managed to raise the sensitivities of the Security and Information Ministry officials, who came to believe more and more that this group must be controlled and silenced. Of course, it took years before a decision to carry out a bloody crackdown against this group was seen to be in the interest of the regime, especially since this group was cautious not to give the security forces any excuses to eliminate them.

With this description, the world, which had only been witness to a one-sided black and white perspective of Iran within its news, was able to hear a different voice from within. From the second decade of the revolution, the world became familiar with active persons who, from within Iran, next to the hidden prisons and Revolutionary Courts, in a language they identified as appropriate, spoke to the people of the world and made them believe that Iran was indeed a country with a multiplicity of perspectives and political ideas. Iran was a country that was familiar with the concepts of modernization. Iran was a country that had long suffered from the deep-rooted tradition of despotic rulers. Iran was a vibrant land where the people were fighting logically and strategically and, by using their past experiences, carried out an effort to free themselves of the traps that had been placed upon their paths in the name of Islam. Iran was a land where the people, despite being dissatisfied with their government, with the passing of time, had been able to present the world with a different image of their country—an image of a people who had a zest for life and for living.

Communication between a wider group of people from within Iran and the outside world allowed the international community to see and understand the reality of Iran as it was—the relationships between the people and their government and among the people themselves. The image of Iran was no longer the sole result of propaganda by the Islamic Republic; rather this new image allowed the world to witness the demands of the younger generation of Iranians as well as their dreams and wishes, and placed the struggles of Iranian women at the center of international news coverage. The reaction of the international community, particularly that of the human rights groups, reflected the messages of experts and activists from within the country, who had seized the opportunity to broadcast and publish their opinions and criticisms through international media sources.

The Iranian Diaspora has played a very important role in informing the world and getting the attention of the international human rights organizations to what was happening in Iran.

9

Under the umbrella of social legitimacy and respect, the thorns that I endured daily were transformed into beautiful flowers. My professional life was continuously peppered with insults and humiliation. One of these encounters was so humiliating and painful for me that it was difficult to overcome, and as a result I took ill.

On that particular day, I appeared in one of the district courts in Karaj—just outside of Tehran—with a client who had been imprisoned by the security forces in Karaj, on charges of corruption in his business. The judge was a cleric and was busy writing up the court proceedings, despite the fact that he had not yet begun the trial. I was sitting next to my client on the front bench in the courtroom. We were discussing my client's case in a hushed tone, so as not to disturb the judge, though he heard our whispering. He raised his head from his papers and stared at us annoyed, and in a demeaning tone, he said: "Woman! Get away from that stranger or else I will arrest you. You are committing a sin in the holy courtroom of the Islamic Republic. Act respectful!"

It was as if the world had turned dark before my eyes. The reproach of the judge was horrific and demeaning. Where could I have objected to this behavior? Without a doubt, the logical place to go with my complaint would have been the bar association, but how? For years following the revolution, the bar association had been stripped of any independence. Its director had been appointed by the judiciary and was loyal to the demands of the clerics who had appointed him. The bar association did not dare defend a lawyer against judges, especially clerical judges.

On the other hand, in order to file a complaint against the judge, I needed my client to testify as a witness. When we left the courtroom I discussed my interest in filing a complaint against the judge with my client. He understood my desire to object to the disrespectful behavior of the judge, but explained that he was in enough trouble already and did not want to upset the judge. I resigned my position as his lawyer and for several months I did not accept any new clients. The only reason I did finally agree to take on new clients, in fact, was because I needed the income.

On another occasion, I had the misfortune of experiencing another dimension of the insulting behavior of the Iranian judiciary system. This time, it was at the office of the prosecutor for the armed forces. I was eating breakfast with my family when the phone rang. The call was from the prosecutor's office of the armed forces, which oversaw cases in which members of the military had been accused. On that day, I was told to appear in the prosecutor's office for questioning as soon as possible. I was about to explain to the person on the other side of the line that according to the law any order to appear in court for questioning needed to be issued in writing, but then I remembered that lawyers did not enjoy any institutional or legal support in this system, so I decided to be quiet instead. I decided to appear in the prosecutor's office and take my chances with whatever the issue was. I realized that remaining in Iran and choosing to practice law required that I endure both insult and gross violation of the law.

I wore a *chador*, an extreme form of *hejab*, as my Islamic dress. This was required gear in the prosecutor's office of the armed forces, as well as the Revolutionary Courts and prisons, for women, even if they were lawyers representing clients. Without of a *chador*, a woman would not be allowed to enter such government buildings. I was forced to confide in my daughter Lily, who was now a teenager. I explained to her that if I did not return, she should understand that I had been placed under arrest. I advised her about whom she should visit and seek assistance from in the case of my arrest. Lily began to cry and from behind her glasses, I could see her tears, which were steadfastly rolling down her face. She saw that I had packed a toothbrush, towel and a change of clothes in my handbag. I also took care to leave behind any materials that could be problematic, like my phone book. I wore my *chador* and got into the telephone taxi, so that I could arrive at the prosecutor's office on time.

Upon my arrival at the prosecutor's office, an armed soldier was assigned the duty of accompanying me to the basement of the building. I waited in the hall. The soldier watched over me, so as to prevent me from escaping, I suppose. I began to laugh at the irony of my situation. Up until that day, I had been the lawyer representing the accused, and now I had become the accused and my situation frightened me to no end.

Finally after three hours of anxious and worried waiting, a short, nervous, angry looking man came down the stairs. He acted as if he had not seen me waiting there. He entered one of the rooms and then in a loud voice called me in to see him. The interrogation started. My interrogator spent the next two hours yelling at me and insulting me. He claimed that I had collaborated with Zionist forces against the military.

As it turned out, the military had signed a contract with a private company, owned by a man by the name of Hakim. In accordance with the contract, Hakim had been awarded prepayment on the deal, but had then failed to come through on his promises. The prosecutor's office was searching for him. In their efforts to find him, they had come to realize that I was the lawyer who had registered the company with the governmental body, "Office for Registration of Corporations." Now they were accusing me of being in cahoots with the Zionist manager of the company, and they claimed that I knew where he was hiding out. The interrogator had decided to treat me as if I were the accused and the one who had committed a crime, and as the interrogation proceeded, it seemed that the number of my charges and crimes also increased.

My accusations, which at first included only corruption, had with the passing of hours turned into political activities against the state. In the end, I was also accused of promoting sexual immorality. The interrogator insisted that since I had been responsible for registering the company, then it logically followed that I had to have been involved in the crime committed by the manager of the company. He also accused me of collaborating with Mr. Hakim in flooding the market with immoral Persian music recorded by Iranian artists in Los Angeles, and he claimed that I was therefore responsible for promoting immorality among innocent youth.

After two hours of these empty accusations, my interrogator told me that I had three days to deliver Mr. Hakim, the manager of the company, to them, or at a minimum give them information on his whereabouts.

I realized then that they did not have any evidence against me, and that they were just trying to terrify me. I also realized that the interrogator was probably just looking for a bribe, which in a business deal of this size could be substantial. I refused to commit to any deal. The interrogator yelled and screamed at me, but I was no longer frightened. He threatened to arrest me. I explained that I had come prepared with my towel and toothbrush. He yelled again, cursing at all lawyers, accusing them of collaborating with corrupt businessmen.

I realized that my interrogator was a weak man and I felt sorry for him. He was trying desperately to make something out of nothing. I remained calm and in a polite tone I explained to him: "Imagine that a criminal escapes from prison. The judiciary officials begin a search to find him. But instead of searching for the criminal, they arrest the clerk who issued his birth certificate. This is what you are doing by interrogating me."

My interrogator was furious. He threatened me and promised that he would charge me with assisting the manager of the company in his efforts to cheat the military. After these threats, he allowed me to leave. I returned home tired and angry. As I arrived home, I could see Lily sitting behind the window of our home, waiting for my return. I could see her begin to smile as I approached. I hugged her and we both began to cry. We promised each other that we would not tell little Azadeh about this event. It would be better to keep it from her.

For a long while after that, I would become frightened and anxious with the ring of the telephone. But the interrogator never contacted me again. He realized that I would not allow him to pull me into his scheme of blackmail and bribery. These people took advantage of the bar association's inability to support and protect lawyers. They realized that after the revolution, lawyers no longer had any support from the law and could not take their complaints anywhere. As a result, interrogators and prosecutors had become accustomed to pressuring lawyers and forcing them to cooperate with them in their schemes of corruption and bribery.

10

I wasn't always humiliated. Sometimes I was treated with respect. In those days, they viewed addiction as a crime. They would keep the addicted individual in solitary confinement or they would take him to a colony, established by the judiciary. At the colony, addicts and drug users were forced into recovery.

One day, the wife of a man who had been sentenced, as a remedy to his addiction, to serve time in the colony for addicts in Semnan entered my office in hysterics. She begged me for help. I was hesitant, but I accepted to accompany her to the Semnan prosecutor's office and should they allow, I agreed to visit with her husband, so that he could sign the necessary papers allowing me to represent him as a defense attorney.

I wasn't hopeful. I just wanted this woman to see with her own eyes that they did not allow lawyers to take on cases such as her husband's. They also did not allow defendants in these types of cases the right to visit with their family members. In fact, having not seen her husband for some time, the woman had come to believe that he had been killed by the judiciary.

We entered the Semnan Judiciary Building wearing black *chador*s, the more formal form of the sheet-like covering that goes over the head and covers the body, with the front remaining open. At the Semnan Judiciary, women without *chador*s were not allowed to enter the building.

I went straight to the office of the Semnan judiciary chief. Contrary to my expectation, all the doors were opened to me and the staff was receptive of my presence. The strategy I had chosen to ensure their cooperation had proved useful indeed. In an effort not to hear an immediate negative response to my requests, I had chosen a strategy that could very well be classified as being in direct contradiction to what was customary for defense attorneys both in Iran and in other parts of the world.

I told the Semnan judiciary chief that the defendant's wife and children were most grateful to the judiciary system for forcing the head of their household to end his addiction. I explained that the whole family was thankful for the benevolence of the judiciary head and were praying for his well-being. My words impressed the Semnan judiciary chief; he was smiling and was so happy indeed that he began tipping his turban in response to my words. In a green pen, he wrote on a piece of paper:

> *In the name of God,*
> *Please arrange for a visit between the defendant and his lawyer.*

I took the letter and left the room with a feeling of elation. But deep down inside I was not satisfied. In my heart, I was cursing my own fate. Where in the world does a lawyer thank the judge for arresting and imprisoning her client? Iran had become the land of the bizarre and I was fighting my descent into this land, as would a psychotic or madman.

In the capital city of Tehran, which tended to be more progressive and open than the provinces, lawyers were not allowed to fight on behalf of their clients. Now here I was in Semnan, in a judiciary based in the provinces—a female lawyer, no less— trying to force my presence in a highly traditional environment that oversaw the addiction recovery camps.

In those days, we were forced to choose unusual strategies for gaining access to areas or information seen as the regime's "red line," or restricted areas. I had become, through many years of practice, an expert at identifying effective and unusual strategies for gaining the sympathy of those who were in power. Those in power would in all likelihood and under normal circumstances not allow a person such as me access to information. Certainly forcing the clerics to accept the presence of a female lawyer in their courtroom was a difficult task, but one worth the trouble.

By the time I discovered all the intricacies of the system and how to manipulate it to my own advantage, I had grown old. I can claim that breaking the ice in the relationship of the cleric judge and female lawyer during the decade that followed the revolution (1980-1990) was indeed a heroic undertaking, and in reality there were only a few women who had chosen to remain active in this field and they conducted themselves and their affairs quietly, without making waves. Certainly these brave women paved the path for others to follow in their tracks.

That day, when the Semnan judiciary chief, allowed me to visit with my client, I felt as if I was the first human to enter outer space and to set foot on the moon and Mars. I was claiming this land, and marking my new territory with my flag of femininity. I valued these small accomplishments as much as life itself, even if I was their only witness. It wasn't important to me that there were no witnesses to my feats, and that no one would ever document them. Just believing that I was able to plant and nurture a small possibility of hope, in that dark and gloomy environment where only ashes could live, I was ecstatic.

I believed that with my *chador*, head scarf and pants, in full Islamic dress, I was able to appear on the scenes of a sensitive moment in Iran's political and social history, and that I was able to maneuver this difficult environment, relying only on my own initiative and internal drive, as if dancing a careful dance on tiptoe. This thought was enough to give me the strength I needed to keep going. I knew that if I could remain on the scene, I would be able to change many of these harsh realities.

In the office of the addict recovery camp in Semnan, the staff looked at me in disbelief. They claimed that this was the first time they had ever seen a female lawyer.

11

Every court session that has to do with divorce or child custody and every trial that deals with the issue of premarital sex or adultery without a doubt reminds me of my childhood nightmares and frightful memories. These events were a replay of the cultural norms and tribal traditions of my city of birth, and I quickly realized that these violent traditions had in actuality been turned one by one into laws that were now being implemented. The first few years of the revolution witnessed the issuing of *fatwa*s (religious decrees) by *mojtahed*s[1], designed to deny women the rights they had acquired through their struggles.

After the establishment of the Islamic Republic based on a public referendum on April 1, 1979, the constitution was adopted and law-making bodies began working actively with the parliament to transform the anti-women *fatwa*s into law. In the beginning, the right to serve as judges, the right to sing (especially as soloists), the right to divorce, the right to dress as they chose (without the *hejab*), the right to be a member of the political staff at the Ministry of Foreign Affairs, and many other rights were denied to women based on *fatwa*s.

Strangely, those issuing *fatwa*s designed to take away the rights women had worked so hard to acquire reaffirmed women's right to vote. They had forgotten that one of the main reasons for their opposition to the Shah's regime was indeed the fact that the Shah had given women the right to vote. The main

---

[1] In accordance with Shiite traditions, *mojtahed*s render an opinion in response to an issue of importance. These opinions, while not taking on a legal form, are adhered to by the followers of the *mojtahed* issuing the opinion. The followers of each *mojtahed* are required to adhere to *fatwa*s, or opinions issued by their leader.

reason for allowing women the right to vote was that religious and political leaders had called upon the Iranian people to carry out their religious duty by voting for the revolution. Women, traditional and religious, who based on religious belief and revolutionary fervor were fully willing to support the revolution, made up a substantial voting block in favor of the revolution and Islamic candidates. The large turnout of women to vote in support of the revolution gave the new government greater credibility and legitimacy in the form of mass support. This mass support allowed the new government to bask in its legitimacy and power and to maintain it.

So, while the *fatwa*s denied women certain rights, such as judgeship, they maintained and insisted upon women's right to vote, and in fact those issuing *fatwa*s restricting women's rights in a number of arenas not only encouraged women to carry out their religious duty by voting, but claimed their right to vote was the most legitimate right of Muslim women. Other *fatwa*s clarified that women were not religiously obliged to be present at the war front, as women's jihad[2] was instead the responsibility of fulfilling their roles as wives. At the same time, the religious leaders called upon women to leave their homes to vote for candidates approved by religious leaders.

In this contradictory environment, the women who had lost their husbands or sons to the war with Iraq were especially honored. The government and propaganda in support of the war placed special value on women who encouraged their husbands and male children to volunteer for the war effort. On the other hand, soldiers returning from the war and during times of peace were sent to big cities and to the northern parts of Iran so that they could identify and arrest women who did not appropriately observe the Islamic *hejab*. These women were arrested and turned over to the judiciary, so that they could be punished in the most violent of manners for their indiscretions. They were flogged for their failure to observe the *hejab* according to the strict codes of the day. Soldiers returning from war had been told that they were obliged to express and then ensure the wishes of their comrades in arms, who had sacrificed their lives for the revolution and for Islam. The wishes of these martyrs were none

---

[2] Holy war or crusade.

other than to ensure women's piety in the form of strict observation of the *hejab*.

In this environment, the female relatives of martyrs, who were in direct contact with the Martyrs' Foundation[3], were transformed into a pressure group that sought to keep women in their rightful place. These women were also put in a position to advocate their own needs through the powerful Martyrs' Foundation. In one instance, their struggle actually had positive benefits for all Iranian women.

During the Iran-Iraq war, the denial of child custody rights to women had created many problems for widows of martyrs, who had lost their husbands to the war effort. The religious leaders who managed the Martyrs' Foundation were faced with a vast outcry by these women. After the revolution, the law had changed to such a degree that widowed women were no longer allowed to interfere in the financial affairs of their children. By relying on this provision in the law, paternal grandfathers had the right to manage the financial affairs of their grandchildren, and often they used their authority to manipulate the finances to their own advantage. Children of martyrs were given a special stipend by the state, designed to cover their living expenses. The law, however, gave their grandfathers the right to manage both the inheritance from their fathers and this stipend, and their mothers had no rights in opposing the decision of the grandfathers. In response, these widows began pressuring the Martyrs' Foundation.

The pressure was so severe in fact that the foundation turned to the judiciary for assistance. The judiciary managed to convince Ayatollah Khomeini to issue a *fatwa* in response. The *fatwa,* later passed into law on July 28, 1985, allowed paternal grandfathers to remain in charge of the financial affairs of their grandchildren who had lost their fathers, whether in the war or not. But the financial right of grandfathers through this *fatwa* was limited only to the inheritance of the child. Any financial assistance provided by the government would be managed by the rightful custodian of the child, who in many of these cases was the mother.

---

[3] The Martyrs' Foundation was set up in 1980 and was charged with tending to the needs and supporting the families of those who lost their lives in the war with Iraq.

This can be classified as the first retreat by the Islamic Republic in its onslaught against women's rights. This retreat was first achieved through the issuance of a *fatwa*, and then through adoption of legal measures and laws, allowing women greater control of the financial affairs of their children. After this event, because of mounting pressure by the public—especially by women, who for over a century had enjoyed active presence in the social, education and employment sectors—the Islamic Republic backed off on several other issues, including a woman's right to divorce, child custody, age of marriage, alimony after divorce, and women's right to be judges.

Despite this, still in the year 2005 when this account is being written, women's rights have not improved under the Islamic Republic enough to be on par with their rights before the revolution. Women judges still don't have the right to sign off on the final verdicts in judicial cases. Women still are not allowed to perform as solo vocalists. Women still don't have the right to represent Iran in foreign affairs as ambassadors. And women still don't have the right to appear in public without the *hejab*.

Additionally, based on the legal measures adopted after the revolution, girls reach the age of adulthood at 9 years of age. This distinction also holds true with respect to legal responsibility of girls. In other words, should girls age9 or older commit a crime, the legal system would be obliged to treat them as adults and the girls would be eligible to be penalized according to penal codes regulating crimes by adults. Given the violent nature of punishments in the Islamic penal system, it is fair to say that women, according to the legal structure of the Islamic government, are denied any immunity as children, and even young female children are threatened by the violent nature of the Islamic legal code.

I struggled in the totality of these contradictions. I listened and watched intently the developments that surrounded me. I closely listened to the Friday prayer sermons of religious leaders, as these indicated changes in the political and social scenes, and especially with respect to the law. I observed closely the developments in the parliament. All that I observed led me to believe one thing: the need to utilize fully any political opening to discuss and bring to light the issue of women's rights. This was especially important as a new lawmaking body, the Expediency

Council, had been added to the legal structure of the Islamic Republic[4]. I realized that positive changes, however miniscule, in the area of women's rights were bound to have significant impact on the daily lives of women.

---

[4] The Expediency Council is a government body that was officially established in 1989, when amendments were made to the constitution of the Islamic Republic (Article 112 of the Constitution of the Islamic Republic of Iran). While in actuality the Expediency Council was established prior to amendments to the constitution in 1989, the amendments created a legal constitutional framework for the creation of this body. The members of this council are appointed by the Supreme Leader of the Islamic Republic and have the potential to adopt secular legislation. The Expediency Council is charged with issuing rulings in cases where the parliament and the Guardian Council have differences on bills approved by the parliament. If a bill is approved by the parliament and amended by the Guardian Council, the parliament must approve the amendments before the law is adopted, or the parliament can, through a two-thirds vote, pass the law in the original form they had approved. In cases where a two-thirds vote cannot be reached and the parliament refuses to approve the changes of the Guardian Council, which are designed to bring the law in line with *Sharia* law, the Expediency Council intervenes. In cases where the parliament and the Expediency Council agree on a law, even if it is not in line with *Sharia* law, the law can be approved. Through this process, laws pertaining to women's rights can be approved and adopted, even if in contradiction to *Sharia* law. Certainly with a sympathetic parliament and Expediency Council, laws could be amended in line with women's modern demands. This could have been an approach with respect to the Sixth Parliament, also known as the Reformist Parliament, during which a number of disagreements on laws were referred to the Expediency Council for intervention. The Expediency Council, however, refused to pass the laws designed to address women's demands, which had been passed by parliament. The hesitation on the part of the Expediency Council to take a progressive approach with respect to women's rights can be explained largely by the fact that the members of the Expediency Council are not elected, rather they are appointed and tend to be conservative and reluctant to steer away from conservative interpretations of *Sharia* law.

12

The Persian language foreign broadcasts and interviews with foreign journalists simply did not seem to have enough of an impact. I was looking for a news platform within the country. I had come to understand that whenever I worked according to a well-devised plan, I was successful in publishing my own thoughts and ideas within Iran. The existing news outlets within the country did not tolerate the ideas of people like me. The weekly *Zan-e Rooz* (Today's Woman), had, like a modern woman who had suddenly become pious and weighted down with the *hejab*, been transformed. The weekly was now under the supervision of the Office of the Supreme Leader. It continued to be published, only now its cover seemed tired and dark.

The rest of the women's publications were published under the supervision of seminaries in Qom or Mashad, and touted an anti-modern and anti-woman line, opposed to women's equality. The myth of Fatemeh, which had been transformed in the patriarchal minds of the men who directed these publications into an order of obedience, contentment and silence for women, was repeated as the underlying premise for all these publications.

I decided to try my luck and republish a number of my articles, which I deemed to be less controversial and which I believed would not arouse the sensitivities of the officials. I gathered the articles for publication in the form of a book. Roshangaran Publishing, managed by Shahla Lahiji, accepted the task of publishing my materials. Of course, the publication would have to first be approved by the Ministry of Culture and Islamic Guidance. My intention in taking up this task was to make sure that I could publish under my own name.

The collection of my articles, titled *The Angel of Justice and Bits of Hell*, passed the many obstacles, and upon receiving approval it was published. This was a major feat and with it, I became accustomed to a new feeling of accomplishment in this dark and heavy environment in which I lived. I felt rejuvenated. Now I understood that if I worked cautiously I could begin writing again. But the world of publishing in the Islamic Republic left much to be desired and my thirst for expressing my ideas fully remained unquenched.

13

As we gained distance from the eight-year war with Iraq, the cultural and publishing sectors were changed and reinvigorated. A ray of light could finally be seen in an otherwise dark cover of the night. The political environment had become more tolerable and new social ideas were given limited opportunity for expression. Newsstands were now adorned with new publications – publications that were long awaited. *Adineh*, *Donya Sokhan* (The World of Words), *Gardoun*, *Sanate Haml O Naghl* (Transportation Industry) and *Safar* (Travel) were some of the new publications that had emerged during this time.

Cyrus Alinejad, a professional journalist from the time of the Shah, who had decided to endure the hardships of the Islamic regime and remain in Iran, began slowly to recruit those who before the revolution had gained some notoriety for their writing, and who had been either denied access to the field after the revolution or had chosen to withdraw. He had a particular talent for starting up impressive and alternative publications at the time of the revolution, and because he was not interested in self-promotion, he had managed to conduct this activity without raising sensitivities.

Cyrus recruited me to work with him on a publication titled *Safar* (Travel), which was associated with the monthly *Sanate Haml O Naghl,* managed by Mr. Amid Naini, a well-respected editor who had been in the business prior to the revolution. I wrote several travel pieces for that publication, from 1988 to 1991. These pieces were based on my travels to more deprived areas of the country, such as the state of Khuzestan after the Eight-Year War, the deprived southern port, etc.

During those days, it seemed that I was not able to find myself easy and clear-cut cases to handle. As a result, and in an effort to make a living, I would accept more difficult cases, which often required that I travel to areas of Iran that were particularly far away and not well developed. These trips afforded me the opportunity to write travel diaries, which were published in *Safar*.

For example, I traveled to Khuzestan, where I wrote about the impact of the war on the region—giving voice to areas of the country that had suffered the disaster of war and were now being looted by government officials. These officials, under the umbrella of "The Task Force to Rebuild War-Torn Areas" and sporting beards, prayer beads and foreheads blackened by prayer stones, were well disguised to carry out their corrupt activities, lining their own pockets with the budgets that were allocated for the reconstruction of areas devastated by war.

The reports I wrote exposed these corrupt officials, under the cover of a travel diary. The economic mafia had come to life and had become powerful with the start of the war and the growth of a black market for foreign currency, and could be readily tied to agents and officials within the Security and Information ministries of the country, who, by providing protection, shared in the spoils of the mafia.

My report managed to disrupt and impact negatively this mafia, which has ever since, under the cover of defending Islamic revolutionary values, followed me and tried to inflict damage upon me. Immediately after I published my travel report, "Khuzestan After the War," the corrupt mafia that had benefited from reconstruction money earmarked for Khuzestan was faced with an upheaval. The report was picked up by the London-based *Kayhan*, which was being managed and run by several exiled writers and journalists. The issue was then immediately taken up by the National Security Council, and "The Task Force to Rebuild War-Torn Areas," which had been directly implicated in the report, issued a statement. The statement was published in the monthly *Transportation Industry* and accused me of slander. This was my first encounter with security forces after the revolution—one that has continued to this day.

With the end of the war, there seemed to be some limited opportunities and openings to discuss some shortcomings of the system. I felt that the political and social environment of the country was no longer pitch black, but was now a shade of gray. During this period—between the years 1991 and 1997—writers and intellectuals experienced several of these openings. But with every opening there was a price to pay. Thieves and political, economic and security power brokers would pressure writers and intellectuals and accuse them of collaborating with and assisting the enemy of the Islamic Republic. All the openings that were created through the efforts of forward-thinking, educated and innovative individuals and moderate religious intellectuals associated with the regime, such as Ataollah Mohajerani[1] and others like him, would quickly become danger zones, where snakes would wait to strike you with their poison.

Within the system, we had no support. The thieves and corrupt power brokers had found us out. They had discovered even my home. I had forever lost my sense and feeling of security. I was constantly afraid. But due to some hidden force from within, which to this day I cannot fathom or explain, I would continue to approach and employ every possible opening that was offered, to advocate for issues I felt were important. I had chosen cautious strategies for criticism, and by so doing, I had been able to minimize the dangers that I faced.

Lily and Azadeh felt frightened every time a government-run publication, such as Iran's national *Kayhan* newspaper, published in Tehran and associated with the Office of the Supreme Leader, or *Kayhan Air*, or the monthly *Sobh* (Morning), made me the subject of their threats, rants and accusations. Perhaps if given the opportunity to judge their mother and her choices, Lily and Azadeh would have come to realize that she was a cruel mother indeed who stole from her children their peace of mind.

---

[1] Mohajerani was a revolutionary who held many government posts from the inception of the Islamic Republic, and who during the reform period (1997) played an important role, including as the minister of culture and Islamic guidance.

14

On February 21, 1993, I participated in a conference organized by four students active in the University Resistance Front, a student organization within the university, at the Faculty of Law at Shahid Beheshti University. The conference, "Women's Social Participation," held at the Allameh Amini Amphitheatre of Tehran University, was one of those openings that I had grown accustomed to utilizing to promote women's rights and alternative ideas. I delivered a paper at the event, titled "The Islamic Penal Code," which addressed the different treatment of men and women under Islamic law. Upon entering the university lecture hall, the organizers, who were standing at the entrance of the hall, pulled me aside. They welcomed me to the event, and added a warning as well:

"This being the first time the issues of inequity within the Islamic Penal Code are being addressed since the revolution, and given the sensitivity of the topic, it is important that you refrain from any expression of emotion while delivering your speech. Please do not display any emotion or create any excitement as you recount the differences in the treatment of men and women under the law. Upon reading your speech, we ask that you leave the podium and we ask that you do not provide your personal opinions or analysis."

I agreed and after delivering my talk I returned to my seat. In response to my talk, the chair of the conference, a woman wearing a *chador*, approached the podium with a defensive stance and began to discuss the points that I had made. She started her points as follows: "A woman is a woman and a man is a man."

She then went on to address several issues that I had raised in my talk. These included:

1- Girls reaching the age of adulthood at the age of 9, under the legal system and within the penal code;

2- Blood money of women being valued at half the blood money for men;

3-The killing of women for proof of a crime not being punishable in some instances, etc.

She explained that these differences reflected the differences that God in his glory had defined between the two sexes. She expressed regret for having been forced to listen to my talk. In so doing, she wanted to make sure that the young, brave students who had organized the conference understood that they should not allow women who believe in the equality of the sexes to set foot into the cultural arenas provided by the Islamic Republic. Islam, she believed, was based on the differences between the sexes, and as such, these rights had been defined differently within the context of the religion. These laws were sacred and were everlasting. They could not be changed.

When I left the conference that day, I could only think of one issue. Why was it that in Iran some groups of women chose to stand in opposition to their own rights? I remembered that after the revolution, in the midst of a time when the displacement of value structures was the norm, I had come face to face with the phenomenon of "women against women."

Iranian women, while being confronted with the reality of the Islamic Republic, had never been coherent in their approach or their voices. They had not chosen a unified response to the anti-woman initiatives and decisions taken up by the state. A large segment of Iranian women, who even during the time of the Shah chose to observe the *hejab*, had been turned into posters children advocating the propaganda of the regime.

They had started demonstrations against women who were opposed to forced *hejab*. Of course, behind the scenes, these demonstrations were organized by men within the ruling establishment, who had at their disposal the facilities necessary to organize such events.

The women who supported the Islamic Regime had many points in common. Besides their *hejab*, which included an overcoat, or manteau, slacks, stockings, headscarf and a black *chador*, these women desperately enjoyed appearing at public gatherings. Mostly they belonged to a social group, which during the Pahlavi era had been under the complete control of either the men in their families or religious leaders. Now after the revolution, religious obstacles to their presence on the social scene had been lifted, with the condition that they continue to observe the *hejab*—a condition to which they were also committed.

Because they felt that the Islamic Republic had afforded them the opportunity to engage in political and social activities, at least at the street level, they refrained for many years from thinking about the legal restrictions placed on women's rights by the Islamic Regime. They were content to just support the war effort by busying themselves with the cooking of food for soldiers. They were content being employed in government agencies without having attained higher education degrees. They were content with their roles as morality police charged with arresting women who failed to properly observe the *hejab*. . They were content serving as officers who checked women's *hejab* and frisked them upon entering government buildings. They were content to spy on their neighbors and provide reports on their morality to the authorities, and assist in the building of cases against those who they perceived to be engaged in anti-regime activities. These activities and incentives, which gradually built their self-esteem, were sufficient in encouraging them to take a defiant position against other women and to work to restrict the rights of women in general and in accordance to what was touted as being Islamic.

Women relatives of political leaders with positions of power within the Islamic government too would appear at conferences such as this one, so as to ensure that these cultural events would not allow for multiple opinions and ideas to emerge on the issue of women. The woman who had spoken in defense of her ideas and in opposition to my paper was one of these women. She was the daughter of one of the well-known ayatollahs in the holy city of Qom. The more exemplary of these women actually had offices and organizations, and on budgets allocated by the government, armed with the excuse of defending the values of Islam and the revolution, they would work to resist any effort designed to ensure equality of rights between men and women. Some even found their way to the parliament.

The next day, when I returned to the conference to listen to other speakers, the young students organizing the event apologized for what had occurred the previous day. They explained that, "We have to work to change the thinking of those who want to ensure they maintain absolute control." These students believed that this group would eventually become more moderate. They also mentioned that the editor in chief of *Zanan* (Women) *Monthly* had asked for a copy of my article.

A week later I received a phone call from the editor in chief of *Zanan Monthly*, Shahla Sherkat. She introduced herself and asked to meet with me. The day I went to her office I found myself surprised. Three women, covered from head to toe in black, were sitting in a small room, behind a single desk. The other rooms of the office were occupied by the men who ran the monthly *Kian*—one of the publications that had emerged after the war, which touted an alternative religious viewpoint that was championed by prominent reformist Islamic thinker Dr. Abdolkarin Soroush.

The women did not have the space necessary for conducting their affairs. With a few potted plants placed outside the room on the balcony, they tried to create a friendly work environment for themselves. Quickly I realized that under their dark *hejab*, these women dreamed of equality between men and women. They had managed with great hardship to publish nine issues of *Zanan*. Within this new publication, they had introduced the issue of women's rights. They had done so from a perspective that advocated equality between the sexes. In support of their ideas, they analyzed differences and offered possible revisions of Islamic doctrine, based on the concept of *Ijtehad*[1]. Their approach was not in line with the thinking of the Islamic Republic.

Shahla Sherkat explained that she intended to publish my article. I was stunned. How was it possible to publish this article? This was, after all, a time when all opposition groups had been crushed and silenced, and all those who had criticized the Islamic penal code had been forced to leave the country or had been forced from the public scene and into their homes.

I was focused and struggling on these questions when a young, small-framed cleric wearing a black turban entered the room. They introduced him as Hojjat ol-eslam Mohsen

---

[1] *Ijtehad* is the practice of providing guidance on religious law. This practice is widely used in Shia Islam, where learned religious scholars adapt religious law to reflect current time and place.

Saeedzadeh. He had not come to the office with a private car and a chauffeur, as was customary of most clerics in those days. Instead he had come from Qom to Tehran by bus, which was the least expensive form of travel in Iran. He carried a small bag containing his belongings.

I collected myself. I pulled up my scarf so that it covered my hair fully. I chastised myself for agreeing to go to the meeting and for entering a new environment that was so unfamiliar for me with such haste. I felt uncomfortable being in this place and did not know what to expect.

The young cleric quickly changed my opinion. It was as if he had read my thoughts. He smiled and explained: "I was forced to change your article. Otherwise, the article would have caused you problems and God forbid you would have been called an infidel."

He pulled the article out of the folder, which had been marked with his notes. I took the article from him and started to read his notes. His handwriting was sloppy, but his thinking, as reflected in the notes, was extraordinarily organized. He had commented on a portion of my writing which read as follows: "Laws are like mirrors reflecting the culture and thinking of humans. Laws should not contribute to the haziness of this mirror and be a source of embarrassment or endanger our national pride."

Mohsen Saeedzadeh had commented by adding the following: "A mirror can brake. Laws can be changed. Islam is the religion of justice. Laws that don't reflect the essence of Islamic justice will out of necessity shatter."

15

The efforts of those brave young students at Shahid Beheshti University in organizing the conference on women's participation, my meeting with the young, forward-thinking cleric at *Zanan Monthly* and the opportunity to contribute to the publishing sector in the Islamic Republic—something that was completely out of reach and unthinkable for people like myself before 1992—incited a passion in me that I could not relinquish easily.

"Something is happening which is not lesser in significance than the Islamic Revolution itself. Cultural and intellectual forces are openly engaged in a challenge with those forces from within the regime. Some have taken a more traditional-conservative stance, while others have become more forward thinking and are actively seeking solutions. Those seeking solutions are consistently looking to new interpretations of Islam. This effort will in the end face substantive consequences and no doubt the supporters of the revolution will in the end come face to face with one another in this battle."

I worked to quiet my passion and focused on the new world that I had discovered—a world that questioned political affairs and developments based on a new interpretation of Islam. For a woman like myself, who had come of age during the time of the Shah, who did not wear the *hejab* by choice and who could be classified as Westernized, the customs and discourse of Islam were not familiar and my migration toward this new approach of resistance and change was not an easy one. But I also had come to understand that a group of people was working to change the blackness that had enveloped their society. They were set on transforming their reality into a green resembling what nature had intended. I joined them in their efforts.

My cooperation in this effort unleashed the bitterness and insults of old friends who had been burned by the revolution. My articles, which were regularly featured in *Zanan Monthly* starting from its 11th issue, sought to provide a critical analysis of women's legal status, based on the accounts of discrimination against women that I had witnessed through my law practice. Through the use of dynamic jurisprudence (*fiq-he pooya*) and by relying on the possibilities provided by the flexibility offered through Shiite *Ijtehad*, Hojjat ol-eslam Saeedzadeh provided an alternative approach to the problems presented in my articles.

His approach was focused on reforming religious interpretations in favor of women. He spoke of the equality of men and women and was not satisfied with anything less. I learned a great deal from Saeedzadeh during the years we collaborated. With his assistance, I learned how to write in the difficult and dangerous environment of the time. I was able to learn a new language and style of writing appropriate for the Islamic Republic—a language and style that minimized the assaults of the clerical establishment.

I was writing on a regular basis, and from the perspective of the equality of rights between men and women, I was engaged in an analysis of the legal structure. Through this venue, I was raising awareness among our readers about the shortcomings of the law. All the while, I made sure that my writings were not slanted in such a way as to be labeled anti-Islamic, as that would have dire consequences in store, promising to destroy me. Secular thinkers inside the country and opposition groups outside the country, which were not only familiar with my past but viewed me as one of their own, began their attacks against me. From their perspective, entering the discussion of women's rights based on religious interpretations was collaboration with the enemy.

These attacks reached a climax at a conference in Los Angeles, at which I was a presenter, organized by the Iranian Women's Studies Foundation (IWSF), in 1990. This was the first time that a women's rights activist from Iran had been invited to present a view of what was taking place in Iran. During this conference, I wore a scarf, as I did not want to destroy all that I had worked for in Iran because of my participation in a conference. The subject of my talk was "Women Enthralled by Presence" and discussed the presence of traditional and religious women in the social and political spheres. These women had received the necessary approval from Shiite leaders in the form of *fatwas*, allowing them to be present in the public sphere, voiding arguments that kept them from this type of participation because of their sex.

The conclusion of my talk put forth the proposition that these same women who had become active due to religious *fatwas*, who had managed to brake down domestic barriers to discover the social and political domain, would eventually realize the shortcomings of the law and demand changes in this area. In this speech I pointed to the fact that some of these women, who could aptly be classified as the elite associated with the ruling families of the Islamic Republic, had begun to discuss the issue of dynamic jurisprudence as a strategy to address and correct inequities in the law with respect to women.

I could barely make my points and had to leave my speech unfinished. The audience was booing me as I spoke and accused me of collaborating with the enemy, the clerics and the Supreme Leader. In response to the cursing and yelling, I had started sweating. A few women who realized the need to ensure my physical safety gathered around me as I stood at the podium, and under their protection, I left the room. The meeting had been sabotaged by extremist opposition of the Islamic Republic. They underestimated the influence and power of the Islamic Republic and believed that through verbal assaults and harassments, and through degradation of religious beliefs, they would be able to damage the Islamic regime and would be successful in toppling the religious establishment. These expatriates had suffered greatly in exile and could not tolerate hearing about the tactics and strategies of activists in Iran, who worked cautiously but steadfastly to create change. They preferred to deny the validity of such strategies and movements.

This was my first bitter encounter with the opposition groups outside of the country—adding to my many difficult and bitter experiences inside Iran. I returned to Iran and began to put behind me the experience I had in California. I continued my legal and human rights activities with greater confidence, but still in the same cautious manner and in the same language that I had come to discover and utilize within the press.

On occasion I would stay up all night focused on writing. I would tackle the subjects of my writing from all angles, predicting all the possible problems that could be associated with the issue that I was presenting, in an effort to ensure that it would not be censored by Shahla Sherkat, the editor of *Zanan*. Sherkat, in those days, given the many restrictions on the press and freedom of speech, was forced to be careful about what she published. One slight mistake would force her to close her publication.

I cannot explain how I enjoyed this life, which was filled with contradictions. It was like an exciting game in precision. Despite the fact that I was careful, *Kayhan Daily*, *Kayhan Air* and the monthly *Sobh* continued and expanded their attacks against me as if moving forward according to a pre-planned agenda. They criticized the editor of *Zanan* for allowing a woman who they classified as sympathizing with the monarchist regime of the Shah and an "anti-revolutionary" to enter the sacred sphere of Islamic publications. These insults and attacks increased with time.

Extremists from all walks of life had made me the subject of their attacks. The extremists outside of the country accused me of collaboration with the Islamists and with Hezbollah, and the extremists inside the country, connected with the ruling elites of the Islamic Republic, accused me of collaborating with and spying on behalf of the United States, and promoting imperialist agendas. All these allegations and accusations made it difficult for me to continue my activities, and on occasion Ms. Sherkat, gripped with fear, would respond to her critics by announcing: "Revolutionary people don't have good writers. We are forced to work with existing writers."

Slowly the secular circles within Iran softened. Perhaps this softening toward me was because of the attacks of those extremist groups inside and outside the country. While criticizing me in their meetings, they would admit that the strategies that I had chosen for addressing issues of concern and raising awareness were indeed correct and they would applaud Shahla Sherkat for daring to print my articles.

The political atmosphere that dominated opposition groups outside of the country also slowly became less radical. Though some remained extreme, others reconsidered their strategies and came to understand that the activists within Iran had the right to utilize whatever approaches they felt necessary to push forth their agendas. Activists inside the country utilized fully all the opportunities that emerged upon the end of the war with Iraq to address and publicize their issues and agendas.

The more moderate opposition groups based outside of Iran, which tended mostly to consist of academics, extended their protection to activists within Iran, regardless of the strategies adopted by these activists in carrying out their agendas. With this development, I was invited regularly to attend and speak at conferences outside of Iran, organized mostly by Iranian academics.

The security forces and Information Ministry officials had become increasingly sensitive to my continued trips outside the country. But, since I had managed to gain a reputation outside of the country and despite the fact that I appeared at these events without the *hejab*—something that along with my attendance and my talks had been added as crimes to my permanent file maintained within intelligence agencies—the security forces realized they could not touch me, at least not easily. In their private circles, the extremist conservatives acknowledged that I had become an issue that should be addressed.

16

My law practice was becoming successful. Clients, both men and women, would seek me out to serve as their lawyer. New clients would especially seek me out after an interview with a foreign Persian language broadcast, or upon reading one of my articles in *Zanan Monthly*. Female clients imagined that, because of the risks I took to expose the legal shortcomings facing women, I had some connections that could help them in resolving their cases. They would rely on me in their quest for justice. They would always enter my office with great hope. But, after an hour or so of consultations and discussions with me, they would leave, their hopes having defected them, as they gained greater awareness of their status under the law, especially Family Law.

One would say: "Help me rid myself of my violent abusive husband."

In response, I would say: "Based on the law, women are not allowed to easily divorce. It takes many years for a successful divorce. In the end the result is uncertain. Your request for a divorce may not be granted. I cannot change the law."[1]

Another woman would say: "Help me in my quest to gain custody of my children."

In response I would say: "I cannot. The law does not allow for this request. Male children can remain in the custody of their mothers until the age of 2 and female children can remain in the custody of their mothers until the age of 7. After that, the father has the sole right to custody."[2]

---

[1] Article 1130 of the Civil Code.

[2] Article 1169 of the Civil Code. This law was amended in 2003, giving some minimal custody rights to women.

Another woman would request: "Help me so that my husband is not allowed to divorce me, after 40 years of marriage. I have spent my youth in his home and now he wants to leave."

I would reply: "I cannot. The law allows men to divorce their spouses at will. The courts cannot limit men's right to divorce. According to the law, men have absolute rights in this regard."[3]

Another woman would say: "At least force my husband to leave me with a home and give me a monthly allowance, so that in my old age, I don't end up homeless and out on the streets."

I would reply: "I cannot. According to the law, a man is not required to provide alimony for his ex-wife after divorce. A woman is only allowed to request her *mehrieh* (bride price), agreed upon at the outset of the marriage, and that is all."[4]

Another woman would say: "My husband has married an 18-year-old girl. He has bought her an expensive and luxurious house in the north of Tehran. Please, could you help me force him to divorce his new bride? Or if not, could you at least force him to buy me and my children a similar house in the north of Tehran? We are living in a dump in the south of the city. Isn't there something that you can do?"

I would reply: "There is nothing I can do. The law allows men to engage in polygamy. This is your husband's right. But if he takes a second wife without the consent of his first wife, this only allows the first wife to seek a divorce. There is nothing else that you can do."[5]

One would say: "My husband has divorced me and I want to marry another man. But, I am afraid that I will lose custody of my children to my ex-husband. Please force my ex-husband to refrain from reclaiming custody of our children after I remarry."

I would reply: "I can't help you in this matter. According to the law, if a divorced woman remarries, she loses custody of her

---

[3] Article 1133 of the Civil Code. This law was amended in 2003 to allow for some reform of the law, but the reform does not curtail the absolute right of men to divorce in practice.

[4] Articles 1078-1101 of the Civil Code and notes 3 and 6 of the Law to Reform Divorce Regulations, adopted in 1992.

[5] Article 1130 of the Civil Code.

children automatically and her ex-husband can reclaim the custody of his children, regardless of their age."[6].

The legal demands of women increased on a daily basis. They believed that I was powerful enough to reverse the laws at whim. They believed that I could convince the judge in court to disregard existing law and rule in favor of my clients, breaking the anti-women laws that were part and parcel of the Islamic legal system. I was struggling desperately with laws that were passed and excused as religious sanction. I was withering under the inconceivable demands women had of the legal system. These challenges impacted me. I was weighted by the magnitude of the realities of Iran and women's position in Iranian society. I realized that my childhood nightmares were coming alive in the form of the law and were being implemented on a daily basis.

I repeatedly resolved to turn away the women who would seek me out hoping for miracles. I wanted to stop accepting cases involving family disputes. Of course, I could never realize these resolutions. Women who were faced with legal problems would hear my words—the words of a woman who would risk her own safety to defend their human rights. In their imaginations, I had been transformed into a "superwoman." They believed that I was capable of defying Islamic *sharia* law. They could not believe that this woman they had become accustomed to hearing on the radio was only an ordinary woman, who had just decided to talk a little. They did not know that, surrounded by the different power centers, security forces and political forces, this woman had no support. They did not realize that she was indeed extremely vulnerable. They could not fathom that this woman, who had chosen to discuss these sensitive issues, would be invited regularly by security forces to clandestine meetings in hotels, where she would be warned to be careful and not to continue with her "extreme" strategies. They could not believe that on a regular basis unknown individuals would enter her office and spend hours interrogating her. They could not believe that this woman they turned to for support would, at the end of each month, have difficulty in paying the rent for her

---

[6] Article 1170 of the Civil Code. Even though the law gives custody of children under a certain age to their mothers, should the mother remarry, she loses custody of any children regardless of age to their father.

home and the rent for her office, and would be forced to turn to loan sharks who had set up businesses in the traditional bazaar of Iran – who were supposedly the pillars of Islamic piety, but in contrast to Islamic beliefs would collect hefty interests on loans paid to those in need.

Women faced with problems would seek refuge in my office and in my advice, and did not realize the difficulties I faced in my double life. They did not realized that I had been strengthened through my efforts at criticizing the status quo, but that in my defense of women's rights within the judicial system of the Islamic Republic I often felt extremely weak and ineffective. My shortcomings in defending the rights of women often left me embarrassed in front of my clients—an embarrassment that cannot be easily described.

17

Azadeh, the little girl who had been born of the tired body of a woman on the verge of menopause, was growing up. Lily had put puberty behind her. She had grown up under the influence of an ideological system, which during its early periods, influenced largely by the war with Iraq, had been extremely violent. This was the environment in which she attended school. As a result, she despised studying and going to school.

The families that were similar to ours with respect to their cultural backgrounds and that benefited from a relatively comfortable financial situation, in the hopes of lifting the spirits of their children and keeping them connected to the modern world, would register them in music institutes or sports programs. The number of these centers had increased considerably after the war. These private institutions required a high tuition, which was often difficult for families to pay. On the other hand, while being private, these institutions were directly controlled by the government and in order to stay in business would have to pay heavy fees to relevant government bodies. Inability to observe "proper Islamic behavior" was the best excuse for closing down these arts institutions or sports centers. There was no uniform or legal definition of "proper Islamic behavior." Government officials charged with oversight of these institutions would use their own definitions of what constituted proper or improper Islamic behavior.

I registered Lily in a gymnastics center, which helped her recover the self-esteem she had lost in her many years of education in public schools, where ideological pressures were the norm. The exercise and physical activity released her pent-up energy and she was able to withstand the pressures she felt at school. At night, Lily would perform gymnastics for us and Azadeh would cheer her on, and as a result of our family interactions, my spirits too were revived.

In those years, one of the daughters of Ayatollah Hashemi Rafsanjani, who could aptly be classified as one of the more powerful religious leaders and founders of the Islamic Republic, by relying on her father's political power, began an effort to open up space for girls' physical education and activity. Faezeh Hashemi, besides benefiting from her father's political power, was also brave and daring enough to tackle this issue. Faezeh quickly distanced herself from other women of the ruling elite, who were satisfied with their presence in the permissible social sphere defined through interpretations offered by religious leaders of the time. Faezeh was young and energetic. The religious ruling elite did not like her and the secular groups made light of her and her efforts. Still, the value and impact of her efforts have yet to be fully evaluated, but it goes without question that she played an important role in breaking down gender barriers in the political sphere of the Islamic Republic.

The second decade of the Islamic Republic is interspersed with the expanding discourse of women's legal rights within the context of dynamic jurisprudence, *Ijtehad* and women's sports. The leaders of the Islamic Republic, under pressure from the world community, were forced to adopt a more moderate stance with respect to laws and reform them to some degree. For example, for divorced women, besides payment of *mehrieh*[1], a dowry agreed upon at the outset of marriage and payable to the wife upon her demand at any time, they instituted another financial payment called *ojrat ol mesl*[2]. They also allowed women to

---

[1] Articles 1078-1101 of the Civil Code.

[2] According to the 6th note of the article on reforming divorce regulations, which was passed in 1992, if a man decides to divorce his wife, without any fault on the part of the wife, he is obliged to pay her an alimony referred to as *ojrat ol mesl*. *Ojrat ol mesl* includes financial reimbursement for the duties performed by the wife during the course of marriage that were beyond her religious duty. The amount of *ojrat ol mesl* is determined by the courts, but tends to be so minimal that it does not allow for the wife to offset living expenses. Additionally, because women have limited rights to divorce, those seeking a divorce without the consent of their husbands usually forgo any monetary payments due to them in an effort to obtain the divorce. This includes both *ojrat ol mesl* and *mehrieh*. On occasion, women seeking a divorce are forced

serve in positions of investigative judges, or advisors to judges within the judicial system[3]. They even added an Advisor on Women's Affairs within the Office of the President. This advisor was named Shahla Habibi and was the first woman to enter the circle of power under the auspices of the Office of the President, within the Islamic Republic.

Despite her position, Shahla Habibi was not allowed to participate in cabinet meetings. The men of the cabinet would not tolerate the presence of a woman within their circles or their meetings. Shahla Habibi was a revolutionary and a religious woman. She observed the strictest form of the *hejab* by wearing a *chador*. She was a young woman who was not allowed to fully assert herself in line with her position. Should she decide to tell of her experience as the first advisor to the president on women's affairs within the political structure of the Islamic Republic, certainly she would shed some light on a noteworthy and key component of transformations with respect to women's rights in the Islamic Republic. I do believe that this woman, despite being religious and a revolutionary, has suffered greatly as a result of her presence in the male-dominated circle of power of the Islamic Regime.

The totality of developments with respect to women's rights moved in a direction that resulted in increased focus on Faezeh Hashemi and her role within Iranian politics. It was rumored that under her *chador* she sported a pair of jeans. It was rumored that Faezeh would appear dressed in the latest Western fashions and in high heels at all-women religious ceremonies and festivities.

---

not only to give up their monetary claims, but they also resort to paying sums of money or giving property to their husbands in an effort to secure his agreement to divorce.

[3] In the year 1995, the law outlining the criteria for the selection of judges, which was passed in 1984 and barred women from serving as judges, was revised. This revision clearly indicates the fact that, under pressure from women lawyers, the government of the Islamic Republic has backed away from its original anti-woman stance. This revision allows for women to serve as investigative judges, advisors to judges, and advisors within the judicial system. As such, women who had been denied positions as judges at the outset of the revolution were once again allowed to take a step in the direction of restoring their rights in this respect. Nevertheless, despite these gains, women are not allowed to make final decisions on court cases and to truly serve on the bench.

Based on her request, in Chitgar Park in Tehran, a special women-only bicycle path was inaugurated. Faezeh had transformed women's right to exercise and physical activity, their right to ride bicycles, and their right to be present in international sports competitions into a religious discourse.

In a precise move, Faezeh replaced the *black habit*, a head covering that many women, especially from the families of the ruling elite, wore under their *chador*s, with a checkered or dotted headscarf. Pictures of Faezeh lightened up the faces of women of the ruling elite, which had been darkened by their black *hejab*. Extremists from all camps began their attacks against Faezeh, who was the daughter of one of the most important and powerful figures of the Islamic Republic. These attacks continued and finally, in a sensitive and important political juncture, succeeded in forcing Faezeh out of the political and publishing scenes that she had managed to penetrate so effectively.

18

My husband Siamak continued to be distraught at his exclusion from the publishing and press scene in Iran. After the end of the war, whenever an organization asked him to collaborate by producing or editing a bulletin or magazine, he would accept the offer immediately. But before long, inevitably, the "Soldiers of Imam Zaman (the Shiite Messiah)" would put an end to his employment. In those days, one of the strategies for eliminating and marginalizing alternative thinkers was through anonymous letters carrying the signature of the "Soldiers of Imam Zaman." These letters would be sent to employers, "exposing" the anti-revolutionary past of the targeted employee. Needless to say, the employer would be frightened and after receiving several of these letters would let the employee go. The writers of these letters usually were informants for the security forces of the regime. This was the strategy they used to exclude alternative thinkers from the publishing and press fields, and they were largely successful in accomplishing their goals.

Siamak was targeted twice by this strategy: once when he worked with a real estate agency and another time when he took on the position of writing and editing the *Shafa* bulletin for the Organization to Support Patients with Kidney Disease. Both times, the Soldiers of Iman Zaman were able to ensure that he was not only fired from his job, but by creating a false case against him they managed to land him in prison and the torture chamber. After a few weeks of not receiving any news about Siamak, who had been serving time in an unknown prison often referred to by intelligence officials as "safe houses," he was driven to an indiscrete location in Tehran and released.

Siamak's mental and emotional state was unstable after both the periods he spent in prison. He would cry often and hard, and this would destabilize our family life. Our children, one a child and the other a teenager, would care for their father. They would not leave him alone and feared that he might commit suicide.

Despite the openings in areas of the press and publishing field after the war, the judicial system of Iran was quickly deteriorating and becoming increasingly closed. Ayatollah Yazdi, the head of the judiciary at the time, decided that the modern judicial system, modeled after the Western system instituted by Davar during the reign of Reza Shah, should be dismantled. As a result, prosecutors and interrogators were removed from the system[1]. He gave judges absolute control and oversight of cases, from their inception to their completion. In essence, this was the death

---

[1] According to the law on the establishment of public and Revolutionary Courts approved in 1994, the public prosecutor's office was eliminated from the judicial system. The note on the 12th amendment of this law reads as follows: "The responsibilities and prerogatives of the public prosecutor will be transferred to the head of judiciary in each province or city." As a result, the judicial system of Iran under the Islamic Republic distanced itself from the pre-revolutionary system and lost the defining criteria of modern judicial systems.

The importance of the prosecutor's office within the modern judicial system lies in its ability to protect the public interest. Its duties are to investigate crimes, pursue criminals and prosecute the accused in line with the best interest of the public. The investigative branch of the prosecutor's office is charged with carrying out investigations, issuing warrants of arrest for the accused, developing cases and referring those cases to appropriate courts for follow-up and trial. In these systems, the investigating judges are differentiated from judges who oversee trials. After the elimination of the prosecutor's office under the Islamic Republic, cases against the accused were referred to and handled from their inception to the court's final decree by either the public courts or the Revolutionary Courts, with the entire process being overseen by the same judge. As a result, this new system ceases to be unbiased and loses the essential component necessary for fairness. The problem is complicated further by the fact that the presiding judge has ultimate control of the case and can deny the lawyer of the accused the right to be included in the investigative process and findings of investigations. Such a system renders the accused helpless and defenseless, allowing the overseeing judge absolute control and power and to use that power to pressure the accused, even through means of torture, to act against his own self-interest, all the while under the guise of the law.

of justice, which had been the hallmark of the Constitutional Revolution in 1906.

In their private circles they claimed that judges, according to *Sharia* law, had absolute rights in deciding cases, and prosecutors and interrogators would only work to limit and obstruct the religious duties of judges. The objections of lawyers and their efforts to retain and protect the judicial system were not successful. Mohammad Yazdi had the final say and he had made his wishes known.

On the one hand, the Islamic Revolutionary Courts that were set up in the first decade of the revolution had worked successfully to create fear among the public, and they had sentenced as many people as they possibly could to death. On the other hand, in the second decade of the revolution, the courts worked to confiscate the property of citizens who had either been accused of crimes or had left the country in fear for their lives.

The Islamic Revolutionary Courts, which to this day continue their activities, do not have any legal basis for existence in the Islamic constitution. Along with these courts, other illegal special courts were established, which mostly worked to crack down on the public.

During these years, it was very common for Iranian families to have a relative in prison or have a family member accused of a crime, and as a result they came under great pressure and scrutiny from intelligence ministry officials. Needless to say, the reality of the time created a lot of stress for Iranian families. We, too, passed our days accustomed to feelings of stress, fear and lack of security. The smallest sound would startle us, exposing our internal sense of paranoia and distress. Of course, we were not alone in our situation. The families of the Mojahedin Khalgh, Socialists, Marxists, government officials within the Shah's regime, those living in exile, and others accused of a crime or being pursued by the legal system lived in a constant state of dread and distress.

19

The scattered members of the Iranian Writers' Society, feeling the time was appropriate, began to reassemble in the years 1991-1996. They moved cautiously to come together and start anew, and began the process of building their membership. Those at the helm of this cultural movement were the remaining intellectuals from the Shah's time, who viewed governance from a Marxist perspective. They put at the center of their agenda support of democracy based on freedom of speech. They had gained experience through their struggles with the revolution. Accused of anti-revolutionary crimes, some of their contemporaries and friends had been executed. Many among them had been arrested and had spent time in prison. Many of their colleagues had chosen to leave the country, preferring exile in Western countries to taking their chances within the Islamic Republic.

Now those who had existed in the margins of the Islamic Republic had reappeared on the scene, and through their collaboration with monthlies such as *Adineh*, *Donya-e Sokhan* (The World of Words), *Gardoun* and *Jame'h Salem* (A Healthy Society) had found another opportunity to assert their presence. In some instances they would take on the arduous task of publishing books, which only through the art of self-censorship could pass the many hurdles that were set up to obstruct free speech. This disarrayed group had found the opportunity seek one another out after the end of the war with Iraq.

The meetings were held in homes of members. They called these gatherings "Consensus Meetings," and they were intended to organize and give shape to the Writers' Society and come to decisions on how to push forth freedom of speech issues. The members of the Iranian Writers' Society felt a great sense of insecurity, which was created under threat of the supporters of the state. The state broadcasting system and dailies such as *Kayhan*

regularly warned that the intellectuals of the Shah's time, supporters of colonial powers, should not be allowed the opportunity
to infiltrate the cultural scene and should not be given the opportunity to assert their existence.

Despite these obstacles, the "Consensus Meetings" continued,
and for a while the intelligence agencies did not feel threatened
by the meetings. Besides the intellectuals who had gained fame
during the time of the Shah, those individuals who had asserted
themselves in the areas of human rights and women's rights after
the revolution, and had gained some fame in this respect, were
also invited to the meetings. Shirin Ebadi, Shahla Lahiji and I
were a few of the better-known individuals fitting this description. We did not have political or organizational experience, but
each of us had gained some level of fame and recognition because of our efforts to advocate for and advance human rights
and women's rights within the Islamic regime. With our inclusion and the inclusion of others like us, new blood was introduced into the Iranian Writers' Society.

Of course, the new arrivals had largely gained their reputa-
tions as a result of the revolution and were unfamiliar with
Marxist ideologies. In fact, they did not adhere to any particular
ideology and were strangers to ideologically-based resistance.
Those in charge of the "Consensus Meetings" could not overlook
the influential presence of these new arrivals in the political and
cultural scenes of the Islamic Republic. Reluctantly they were
forced to open their doors to feminists and human rights activists. Before the revolution, the women who advocated on behalf
of women's rights did not have access to intellectual circles. But
activism on behalf of women's rights and human rights after the
revolution had been recognized as a legitimate activity in opposition to the state. Perhaps this was because anti-women policies
had become the hallmark of the Islamic Regime, and women's
rights activists, having taken on the Islamic regime head on,
were in a position to start, impact and contribute to opposition
movements.

Whatever the factors, the ice that separated these two groups
was finally thawing. The pleasure of connecting with secular
thinkers was immense. It had been many years since these secular-minded individuals could easily engage in discussions with
one another. It felt like a huge burden had been lifted, and they

had finally been allowed to voice their opinions, even if in the isolation of their own meetings.

Two years into these meetings, a public letter with 134 signatures, including mine, was issued. The letter came to be known as "Letter 134" and was faxed to writers' organizations in the West. The letter was short and effective.

October 15, 1994
Tehran, Iran

We are writers...
But problems which have arisen in the contemporary history of our society as well as other societies have distorted the image of the writer in the eyes of the state, certain sectors of society and even in the eyes of writers themselves.

Consequently, the identity of the writer, the nature of his/her work, and even the collective presence of writers have all been subjected to undue attack.

It is our duty, therefore, as writers of Iran, to explain the nature of writing as a cultural enterprise, and the reason for our collective presence.

We are writers.

By this we mean that we write our feelings, imagination, thoughts and scholarship in various forms and publish them.

It is our natural, social and civil right to see that our writing—be it poetry or fiction, drama or film-script, research or criticism or the translation of works written by other writers of the world—reach the public in a free and unhampered manner.

It is not within the capacity of any person or organization to create obstacles for the publication of these works, under whatever pretexts these may be. Free judgment and criticism, however, are open for all, after the publication of such works.

When the struggle against the obstacles of writing and publishing exceeds our individual power and capacity, there remains no other alternative for us except to encounter these difficulties in a collective professional manner.

In other words, in order to achieve freedom of thought, expression and publication and in order to campaign [against] censorship, we have to exert our efforts together.

We believe, therefore, that:

Our collective presence with the aim of crating a professional writers association in Iran is the guarantee to our individual independence, because a writer should be free in the creation of his/her work, the criticism and analysis of works by other writers, and in the expression of his/her beliefs. His/her cooperation and agreement with the common problems of all writers do not mean that s/he should be held responsible for the individual problems of other writers.

Similarly, the responsibility of personal, political and social thoughts and actions of each writer belong only to that particular writer.

Nevertheless, the writer here is looked upon not because of his profession as a writer, but because of his alleged association or assumed connection with parties, groupings or factions; judgment is passed upon him/her on the basis of these assumptions.

As a result, it seems that the collective presence of writers and cultural-professional organizations will be seen as equivalent to membership in a political party or advocacy of a particular political agenda.

Governments and their dependent institutions and groupings customarily evaluate a writer's work on the basis of their own bureaucratic mechanisms and policies. Relying upon these arbitrary tools, they attribute the collective presence of writers to certain political tendencies or to internal and external conspiracies.

Certain individuals, institutions and groups related to the government even exploit these arbitrary interpretations in order to vilify, humiliate, and threaten writers.

We hereby emphasize that our principal goal is the removal of all obstacles on the road to freedom of thought, freedom of expression and freedom of publication; we emphasize that any other interpretations of our aim would be incorrect and stress that the responsibility of these misinterpretations lies with those who have wrongly identified our goals.

The responsibility of any text lies with the person who writes and signs it freely.

Therefore, the responsibility of whatever is written and signed and published inside or outside Iran, in agreement or disagreement with us—the writers of Iran—lies only with those who have signed such a writing.

There is no doubt that the right to analyze and evaluate all works of literature and scholarship is one that all should enjoy; the critical analysis of works by writers is the prerequisite for the promotion of national culture.

Spying into the private life of a writer as justification for the criticism of his/her works is tantamount to intrusion into his/her privacy; condemning a writer on the basis of his/her moral and ideological convictions is contrary to the principles of democracy and the ethics of writing.

Defending the human and civil rights of every writer is, under all circumstances, the professional duty of all writers.

To sum:

Our collective presence is the guarantee of our individual independence; the private thought and action of one writer has nothing to do with the assembly of writers; this is what we mean by the democratic outlook of an independent professional organization.

Although it may seem a tautology, we reiterate: We are writers; look upon us as writers; consider us collectively as the professional presence of Iranian writers.

The publication of this letter worldwide was successful in eliminating the little security that the signatories enjoyed in Iran. The letter became a hot topic for intelligence ministry officials, who felt that the individuals who had signed it had endangered national security. The organizers of the "Consensus Meetings" were called into court one by one and were interrogated and threatened by intelligence ministry officials. The government-run publications and press started insulting and slandering those who had signed the letter, and cases were built against each of us. Several people, under threat, were forced to rescind their support of the letter. The signatories and their families were in great danger. The world community was stunned by the letter. No one truly believed that the absolute control of the ruling clergy could be shaken by a lone letter signed by a number of secular thinkers. But it was true. The Islamic Republic had been shaken and its absolute control weakened.

20

The results of the fifth round of parliamentary elections in 1996 introduced the clerical establishment to a new phenomenon and forced them to ponder developments. As it turned out, as was rumored, the votes cast for Faezeh Hashemi in the parliamentary elections were higher in number than those cast for Ayatollah Nategh-Nouri, who was a powerful religious leader. Before the results of the election were officially announced, the clerical leaders began discussions within their ranks on how to respond to this unexpected development. They decided to announce that Faezeh Hashemi had received fewer votes than her competitor, Ayatollah Nategh-Nouri. It had been rumored that Ayatollah Hashemi Rafsanjani, Faezeh's father, played an important role in reaching this decision. The clerics in their entirety felt worried about the fact that a woman had received more votes than a powerful and well-known ayatollah in the elections, and were reluctant to announce this development publicly. This was a new and unprecedented development in the electoral history of the Islamic Republic.

Only a small percentage of the Iranian public participated in the parliamentary and presidential elections of the Islamic Republic. Usually those who participated not only supported the revolution and the Islamic regime, but also voted disproportionately for clerics. The silent majority did not enter the election scene. This time, the supporters of the regime had elected a woman in Tehran, a city with great political significance, as it was not only the capital of the country and a power center, but also home to a large population of about one-sixth that of the country. The voters in Tehran had preferred Faezeh to a well-known and powerful cleric. This development was so new and unusual that it produced fear among the clerical establishment.

I discovered an important message in this development, which I discussed in an article titled "Women on their Way." The article was published in *Zanan Monthly*. In my opinion, society, even that segment of society which readily participated in elections, had exhibited a readiness to distance itself from the clerical establishment that had governed the country between the years 1979 and 1996. The public's preference for a young woman over a powerful cleric was proof enough. Even the segment of the society that supported the regime had new demands of the system and had grown tired of the clerical leaders that sought absolute power.

Through analysis, and based on beliefs and justifications in line with the will and desire to not only save face but to ensure the legitimacy of the clerical establishment, it was announced that Nategh-Nouri had received the highest number of votes in Tehran. It was also announced that Faezeh received the second highest number of votes. But even with this solution, they were not able to prevent the emerging political movement that sought to impact the system through elections.

Faezeh was not able to utilize her opportunity fully as a member of parliament. In this new role, Faezeh did not continue with her daring strategies for change that often broke with tradition. Perhaps surrounded by the conservative majority of the Fifth Parliament, she lost her nerve. Few women of the Fifth Parliament were able to stand up to the conservatives who promoted an anti-woman agenda. As a parliamentarian, Faezeh Hashemi ignored the demands of her voters and their expectations. The voters looked to Faezeh to advocate for women's rights by using the podium at the parliament to make innovative and exciting speeches critiquing the status quo. She had managed to expand discussions about gender within ruling circles under the pretext of women's right to physical activity. With the support of her father and his power, she had managed to remain on the political scene, but was not able to use the platform afforded her as a member of parliament in a manner in line with the expectations of her voters. After this achievement, Faezeh quickly lost her appeal. Unfortunately, the Fifth Parliament came to be known as a parliament that not only refused to reform laws in favor of human rights, but as a parliament that adopted laws in favor of human rights and women's rights abuses.

21

I enter the building of the prosecutor's office in Ark Square in Tehran. Before the revolution this building housed the National Radio Broadcast. Some of the public criminal courts are housed in this building. I enter the office of the judge assigned to the case I am handling. I have an appointment with the judge so that we can review the letters written by an old woman who has been murdered. The letters are to be used as evidence incriminating the murderer in this case. While being simple and clear-cut, the case is also complicated, as the murder victim is of the Bahai faith.

I open the file and turn over one of the letters to the judge. The judge, an educated young man familiar with the customs and workings of the judicial system and judicial review, extends his hand to receive the letters. In a sudden move, though, he retreats and pulls back his hand. He grabs a tissue and uses it to hold the letter in such a manner so as not to actually touch the paper on which it has been written. I am surprised by this behavior, but realize the reason for the judge's actions. The judge believes that Bahais are impure and the hands of a Muslim believer should not be contaminated by a letter written by a Bahai woman. My heart sinks. How can a closed-minded judge review and oversee this case objectively and punish the criminal who murdered this innocent woman?

Upon leaving the court, I contact my clients immediately. My clients are the daughters of the murdered woman. One lives in Germany and the other lives in the United States. In fear for their lives and safety and in fear of the intelligence and judicial systems in Iran, which place no value on the lives of Bahais, these girls have chosen to leave Iran. They refuse to travel to Iran even in their quest for justice in the murder of their mother. According to an interpretation of the legal system in Iran, Bahais are viewed as *mahdur ol-dam*,[1] and as such their murder holds no legal reprisal, or punishment, especially if the murderer is a Muslim.

The old lady is a Bahai who was not willing to leave Iran after the revolution to join her children in exile. With great difficulty and stubbornness she decided to stay in Iran and protect her home and orchard in Zafaranieh, a neighborhood in the northern part of Tehran, from the encroaching hands of the Revolutionary Courts and prosecutor's office in charge of confiscating property.

For 20 years, this old woman was involved in a legal battle with the prosecutor's office at the Revolutionary Courts and despite its many threats, the prosecutor's office was unsuccessful in forcing this old woman from her home and country, relinquishing the property to the Islamic coffers of the Islamic Republic. She insisted on the right to own property and continued her struggle against this unjust regime, until one day a man who probably had a collaborative relationship with the prosecutor's office, along with his family, moved into her home as tenants. At first the woman felt comforted by the present of her tenants. After a short while the tenant began to implement his assignment. His 18-year-old son, who had befriended the old woman, visited her in her home and asked to borrow a few books on Bahaism. The next day the tenant turns over these same books as proof of criminal behavior on the part of his landlady to the Revolutionary Courts. He included a letter of complaint to the prosecutor's office explaining that his landlady was promoting the Bahai faith and was trying to convert his 18-year-old son into a Bahai.

---

[1] *Mahdur ol-dam* refers to someone who is subject to bloodshed with impunity. In other words, the murderer of persons subject to bloodshed with impunity would not be subject to legal recourse. One of the most dangerous effects of *Sharia* on the legal system has been the use of the term "bloodshed with impunity," or *mahdur ol-dam*, in several articles of law, including Article 332 of the Islamic Penal Code, Note 2 of Article 295 of the Islamic Penal Code. At the same time, the definition of exactly who is considered to be *mahdur ol-dam*, or subject to bloodshed with impunity, creates a legal vacuum that generates terror. The laws go to great lengths to protect the rights of those who commit murder of a person proven, whether in advance or de facto, as being subject to bloodshed with impunity or *mahdur ol-dam*; yet at the same time the laws fail to protect the rights of murder victims and their families in these cases.

The old story takes a new twist. The old woman is accused of promoting the Bahai faith, which carries a heavy penalty. As a result, the court's verdict calls for the confiscation of her property. The prosecutor's office and its agents, who were supporting the tenant, increase their pressure on the old woman in the hopes that she will grow tired and give up, vacating the property. But she continues to resist the pressures and remains in her home. The prosecutor's office, in its benevolence, allows the old woman to remain in her own home, but confines her to only one room in the house. The rest of the property is turned over to the tenant, who from then on is recognized as the tenant of the prosecutor's office, the new landlord of the property. The tenant is not required to pay rent to the new landlord. The old woman continues to go to the prosecutor's office in the hopes of re-claiming her property, but to no avail. The prosecutor's office lays full claim to the property, and agents of the prosecutors hope that the old woman will die under pressure of harassment from their tenant. Eventually the old woman realizes that they are planning to kill her.

She writes about 20 letters to her daughters explaining her circumstance. She explains that she is fearful about the outcome of her situation and that her tenant is charged with murdering her. The insistence of her daughters urging their mother to leave the country is of no use. One day her body is discovered in the same room she had been limited to in her house. She had been strangled with her own scarf. They take her body to the coroner's office in the hopes that her body would go unclaimed. The daughters of the victim contact me and plead with me to take on the case. They sign over power of attorney to me so that I can, with the assistance of their Muslim relatives, claim the body so that the dead woman can receive a proper burial. The daughters are distraught and emotional and beg me to take on the case so that they can put their mother to rest, and so that they, too, can have some peace.

I go to the coroner's office. They refer me to the courts. The courts refuse to take responsibility. They are reluctant to turn over the body of a murdered Bahai woman. I continue my in-quiries, going back and forth from the coroner's office to the courts for 10 days. Finally I succeed in claiming a blackened and bruised body. They want me to identify the body. But how? I had never seen the woman. I ask the woman's son-in-law – a wealthy Muslim man who has come to Iran for a few days to take care of his property – to come to the coroner's office to identify the body of his mother-in-law. He yells at me. He is afraid that the agents of the prosecutor's office will find out that he is married to a Bahai woman and, with this excuse, move to confiscate his property as well. I ask a friend who is a distant relative of the son-in-law for assistance. He agrees and we go to the coroner's office so he can identify the body and sign the necessary documents. All of a sudden, two people appear at the coroner's office. They claim that they are associated with the office of Bahais and are in charge of burials. They provide me with identification, which bears the seal of the Revolutionary Courts. They pay the burial fees and I accept the body. The two Bahai officials explain privately that the international Bahai community has requested that I accompany them to the graveyard so that the body of this woman is not stolen en route. We enter Khavaran Cemetery. For years this graveyard has been called "the land of the damned." It is the burial ground for Marxists and those opposed to the Islamic Republic. I look at the graves. The gravestones have been destroyed by extremists who have taken to beating and threatening the families of those who have been buried here. The graves are decorated with seashells, which wash away into mud with the slightest rain.

I pass the unmarked graves. I enter the funeral home, where the bodies of the dead are washed before burial. There are a few people present, who have taken to filming the event. I am there as a silent witness. These people take pictures and film the body, which has acquired a stench and was blackened. They say that up to that point, 80 Bahais had disappeared, but their bodies had never been found. According to the Bahai officials, this was the first time that the body of a murdered Bahai had been discovered. They say that the international Bahai community has thanked me for my assistance in this case.

Ashamed of being a Muslim, I leave the graveyard. The next morning I continue following the case, without any payment and without any hesitation or interruption. After about two years, the same judge who refused to hold the letter from the old woman makes a ruling on the murder case. The ruling finds the tenant of the murdered woman, accused of the crime, innocent. I object to the ruling. To date, at the time of writing this account, the Supreme Court has refused to render a final decision on this case. It seems that this has been an intentional strategy chosen by the Supreme Court to prevent the international Bahai community from using the ruling in this case in their information-sharing efforts regarding the problems faced by Bahais in Iran.

I later heard that the Muslim son-in-law of the murdered woman, the same one who was too frightened to come to the coroner's office to identify her body, had sought the assistance of well-connected people working with the judiciary and was trying to reach an agreement with the prosecutor's office at the revolutionary court, to divide the property between himself and them. The son-in-law had claimed that he was able to convert his Bahai wife to Islam, and this was the excuse used to win him favor within the judiciary. I have heard he didn't get any results and was not successful.

From my perspective, the old Bahai woman was a rare human rights activist who, while surrounded by criminals, continued to defend her own rights and the right to her own property, and for nearly two decades she was able to withstand the pressure of the judiciary and its agents. The history of the Iranian judiciary and court system can attest to the existence of many such nameless heroes. I believe that the human rights movements sprout from the nourishment of their blood, and Iranians from all walks of life, believers in different religions or those with differing political leanings, take care to protect these buds that will grow to cast their benevolent shadows on all of humankind. The Iranian government is not able to avoid the growth of these sprouts. The professional life of lawyers, however, even in the second decade following the revolution, is witness to these amazing acts of heroism. We are witnesses to such immense and painful acts of injustice, that we are unable to expose them.

In all of my professional experience, the conclusion drawn is that the lawmaking mechanism in Iran is weak. This mechanism cannot amend the undemocratic laws or pass more democratic laws. In short, I came to the realization that the lawyers in Iran cannot insist on the international basics of human rights in the Iranian courts and thereby protect the citizens' lives, property and respect without changing the Constitution. In the Islamic Republic's Constitution, the only basis and source for legislating is the *sharia* and Islamic law.

22

It was a hot summer afternoon in the year 1996. Along with five other writers, who were members of the Iranian Writers' Society, I had attended a dinner party at the home of the cultural attaché of the German Embassy. We were at the dinner table when suddenly a group of Intelligence Ministry agents stormed the house and yelled, "What are you doing in the home of this German spy?"

Simin Behbehani, Houshang Golshiri, Mohammad Sepanlou, Faraj Sarkouhi, Roshanak Dariush and I were guests at the home of the cultural attaché. A few of these intruders were carrying video cameras on their shoulders and were filming us throughout the encounter. They ordered us not to move from our seats, so they could capture the evidence against us on film. What was the evidence against us? What was the crime that was being committed at the dinner party?

According to the law, which after the revolution had been interspersed with Islamic punishments, our behavior at the party was indeed criminal. The reasons included the fact that the three women at the party had not observed the Islamic *hejab* and were sitting at the dinner table next to men. Simin Behbehani, a renowned Iranian poetess, Roshanak Dariush, a writer and translator of German texts, and me. We had abandoned the confining Islamic dress, and like the era before the revolution, we were talking with our host and the other guests. In this state, and according to the Islamic law of the land, we were committing the following three crimes:

1- Appearing without *hejab*, which was punishable through flogging (10-74 strikes), imprisonment and fines;

2-Mingling, talking and laughing with the opposite sex, which was viewed as a crime and punishable by flogging (74 strikes); and

3- Consumption of alcohol, which was punishable by flogging (100 strikes).

All three of us women were around 50 years of age. The men who had stormed the room and were accusing us of loose and immoral behavior were around the same age as our children. We wanted to recover our overcoats and headscarves from the coat rack at the front door. We wanted to cover ourselves in our Islamic dress, so that perhaps our crimes could be minimized.

They ordered us to remain in our seats so that they could film us from all angles, especially capturing the fact that we were there without proper Islamic dress. The cultural attaché was stunned and confused. He was taken by surprise. It was a completely unexpected development for him. He was asking his interpreter to let him know what was going on. I was seated between Houshang Golshiri, who was a novelist, and Faraj Sarkouhi, who was the editor of the monthly *Adineh*. Wine glasses filled with white and red wines could be seen next to each of our plates. Given the fact that the consumption of alcohol was a crime, proof of our criminal activity would mean 100 strikes with a whip. There was no getting around this punishment. I examined this scene from a lawyer's perspective and realized that based on the crimes we had committed we would be subject to 284 strikes by a whip. I wondered which of us could physically survive this intense flogging. Needless to say, these crimes were minimal as compared with the real crime of espionage and actions against national security, which were obviously part of the agenda of the intelligence agents.

But the real fear was the realization that this was part of a larger project that was being implemented by the intelligence forces and was designed to crack down on the individuals who had signed "Letter 134." I was familiar with these types of projects. Sometime prior to that night I had seen a program on the government-run television, which had claimed that all the modern intellectuals since the time of the Constitutional Revolution in 1906 were agents of the British Empire or cronies of Western governments. This program was broadcast in the form of a weekly series called *Hoviat*, or *Identity*. Now it was clear that they wanted to utilize the same strategy to attack and marginalize the remaining intellectual thinkers, whom they saw as opponents of the regime. The dinner party was an opportune moment for doing just that.

It seemed that the German cultural attaché did not have the experience necessary to work effectively in Iran. He had failed to formally inform the Ministry of Foreign Affairs of the location of his home, which was required of diplomats. As a result, his home did not benefit from diplomatic immunity and the Intelligence Ministry agents had taken advantage of this fact. They had learned of the dinner party through our telephone conversations, which were wiretapped and monitored.

After they had finished filming us, they allowed us to wear our Islamic dress and to contact our families. We were instructed to tell our family members that the party had continued late into the night, but that we were on our way home. I called home. Lily answered the phone. She sounded half asleep. She gasped and said, "I understand."

Lily had sensed the danger. When I arrived home from the detention center, the location of which I was not aware, I recounted the story for the members of my family. I explained that from then on, our private life no longer existed. I made my husband Siamak and Lily understand that they had to be aware of their activities. I warned them that there were dangerous consequences awaiting me and the others who had signed "Letter 134." I warned that they needed to be careful from then on. With this development, all aspects of my life—social, personal and professional—were under threat. The sense of security had forever abandoned our household. Later I found out that even Azadeh's conversations were recorded and monitored with the intention of building a case against me.

I had turned into a mother who had robbed her children of a sense of security, and had instilled in them a sense of fear. These worries even denied Lily the right to hold parties for her friends. We were afraid that intelligence ministry agents would storm into our home during one of these parties and, with the excuse of safeguarding religious morals and values, arrest our guests. There always seemed to be an unmarked motorcycle with no license plate roaming the streets around our home and my office, and this frightened my children and prevented them from inviting their friends to our home.

Lily was 20 years old. She was a student of law at Shahid Beheshti University. She suffered more than Azadeh. She wanted to feel young and enjoy herself, and at a minimum she wanted to feel free in her own home. But she couldn't. As a result, she would host parties at the homes of friends, where she felt safer. Slowly, Lily's connection to our family was weakened. She developed friendships with individuals and families who were strangers to the world of politics and the consequences of political activism. In their midst, Lily became accustomed to the pleasurable feeling of safety. Siamak and I became accustomed to the bitter feeling of loss—the loss of Lily.

23

Intelligence agents had started visiting me at my office. One day they would show up claiming to be conducting an investigation. Suspicious looking agents from the office of "Amaken"— which had jurisdiction of public spaces and reported to the prosecutor's office about suspicious political or moral behavior—would enter on another day, holding a warrant from the prosecutor's office, and would ask me questions about my relations with foreign embassies in Tehran. On another day, security forces from the office of passport control would enter my office and ask me all sorts of personal questions. On occasion, they would come disguised as clients so that they could have access to the comings and goings in my office.

Finally one day a giant of a man, who was an agent of the Information Ministry, entered my office. He called himself Habibi. When I asked him for identification, he replied, "Aren't the two agents standing in the street and the agent standing at your front door, charged with surveillance of your office, identification enough?"

In a swift reflexive move, he showed me his gun, which he carried hidden on his person. That day is forever marked in mind as the day that destroyed all the walls protecting my personal, social and family lives.

Mr. Habibi was informed of the most personal of our phone conversations with friends and loved ones. Every time he set up an appointment to interrogate me at the office, he would do so by telephone and would order that only one family member could be present during the interrogation. He would also explain that during the interrogation, which took place in my office, no one was allowed to answer the phones or to make a phone call. Likewise, we would not answer the door and my office would be closed to my clients during the course of my meeting with Mr. Habibi.

On those days that Mr. Habibi would come to my office to torture me with all kinds of irrelevant questions that seemed to have no end in sight, my personal and professional lives would take a break. It was as if they had convened the revolutionary court in my place of work. Mr. Habibi, on the other hand, would tell me of the favor he was doing for me. He would claim that it was in my best interest to meet with him in my office, rather than be called into his. This, according to Habibi, saved me some unpleasant embarrassment.

Mr. Habibi continued with his visits for about a year. In one of his last interrogation sessions, he warned me that there was a possibility that some believers upset by my beliefs might want to assassinate me. He warned that I should be careful and should call them immediately should I receive an unmarked package from an unknown source.

He also reached into his pocket and took out a picture of Lily when she was 2. He handed the picture to Lily, who was present with me at the interrogation. Lily and I, stunned and speechless, looked at one another. Mr. Habibi explained that our phone had been tapped for months. As a result, Lily's conversations with her friends were also recorded. Information Ministry agents, realizing that Lily had broken up with her boyfriend, had taken it upon themselves to retrieve this picture of Lily, which she had given him as a keepsake. It seemed that after their breakup, Lily had repeatedly asked her boyfriend to return the picture, but he had refused. Habibi and his colleagues decided to teach the boy a lesson. They went to his home and through physical force they had made the boy bring them his picture album, so they could retrieve Lily's picture.

This account was too much to bear for both Lily and I. It seemed that after that meeting, Lily slowly withered away. She confided that she felt as though she had been prancing around exposed and naked in front of Habibi and his colleagues for months. Later on I found that during their visit with Lily's boyfriend, they had forced him to write a note claiming that I had been spying on behalf of foreign embassies in Tehran.

This development left me mentally distraught, and left Lily with a sense of emotional instability. She turned to the same young man for support with whom she had broken up. In the same meeting, Habibi warned Lily that, given the fact that she had not adhered to Islamic codes of conduct with respect to her personal relationships, she should be careful about her behavior at the university. Specifically, he warned that she should not try to show off at law school by asking professors difficult or controversial questions, giving speeches or expressing her ideas. He also explained that they had received reports that Lily had begun organizing female students who respected her mother at the university. The reports indicated that Lily intended to disrupt the university environment by compelling these students to object to Islamic laws.

These security-oriented measures created in my daughter, who loved Iran with all her heart and who had intended to continue in the path of her mother, a state of emotional instability. Lily finished her undergraduate degree reluctantly. Her grades began to slip after that meeting. She was stubborn and blamed me for the invasion of her personal life. She turned her back on me. After that she spent a lot of time around the Canadian Embassy in Tehran. In the end, she succumbed to escape the country she had once loved so dearly. She migrated to Canada and left Iran forever.

24

Lily wasn't the only one frustrated by the intrusive behavior of
the regime. The large majority of the Iranian people had grown
frustrated with the system and they were approaching a boiling
point. It was difficult for the Iranian public to tolerate the continued presence of morality police and patrols who would regularly
arrest citizens in hordes at shopping centers, street corners,
automobile check points and other public gathering places, with
charges of inability to observe appropriate *hejab*, mingling with
the opposite sex, listening to music, etc. On the other hand,
problems such as lack of access to water, electricity or housing
for those living in the outskirts of Tehran added to these tensions. There were sporadic protests in cities such as Islam Shahr,
Qazvin and a few others. The regime kept receiving warning
signs.

The *Ruhaniyun-e Mobarez* (roughly translated as "Resisting
Clerics")[1], a group of clerics with leanings to the religious left,

---

[1] This group was formed after the revolution and some of the members
played a supporting role in the taking of American hostages at the U.S.
Embassy in Tehran. Economically, they tended toward a socialist ideology, but on social and political issues they were extremists, especially
in dealing with opponents of the regime. They also touted an extreme
anti-American platform. While their ideas and ideology were not necessarily reform-oriented or forward thinking, because they were marginalized by *Ruhaniyat-e Mobarez* (roughly translated as right-religious
clerics), who controlled the government after the death of Khomeini,
they began to criticize their political rivals. Gradually this group was
transformed into an opposition group from within the system. Eventually, with the inclusion of and through collaboration with younger con-
tributors, *Salam Daily* turned into a platform advocating more progressive, reform-oriented ideas. Because this was the only venue through

who had been marginalized by the more conservative clerics after the death of Khomeini, began utilizing a platform provided by the daily publication *Salam* to report on the broad dissatisfactions faced by the public, and to advertise its viewpoints. The policies of President Hashemi Rafsanjani, who was in his second term, were severely criticized by the editors and writers of *Salam Daily*. The political, economic and other failures of the government were regularly reported on by *Salam Daily*. Up until the start of the reform period in 1997, *Salam Daily* was the only alternative press venue that, by relying on the revolutionary power of anti-U.S. figure Hojjat ol-eslam Mousavi-Khoiniha, who headed the paper, reported on the needs, demands and problems of the Iranian people.

Abbas Abdi served as the editor in chief of the paper. He was the young man who had played a major leadership role in taking the American Embassy and its diplomats hostage at the outset of the revolution in 1980. He was also a leader of the anti-U.S. students, who called themselves the "Followers of the Imam." Mousavi-Khoiniha in those days headed the "Followers of the Imam." As such, the history of political activism of these two persons was rather clear. Now Abdi had chosen to capitalize on his political history to expose the main problems of the government of Hashemi Rafsanjani, and all that took place behind the closed doors of his government, which the propaganda machines worked hard to keep hidden.

During the presidency of Rafsanjani, the Information and Security ministries imprisoned Abbas Abdi for 11 months. After his release, he continued his activities as the editor of *Salam* and continued to expose all that took place within the Rafsanjani government. In the years before 1997, the "Resisting Clerics" were able to connect with other reform-minded groups and begin a process of advocacy in cultural and even intelligence centers. They found the political situation to be unpalatable and they saw the dissatisfaction of the people as a major source of concern and threat to the existence of the Islamic Republic.

In the advocacy process, the monthly *Kian* and its managers, who for the most part advocated an alternative religious interpretation, along with Saeed Hajjarian and his sympathizers had

---

which the ruling elites were criticized, *Salam* managed to gain vast support among intellectuals and even secular-minded Iranians.

opposed a plan to physically eliminate secular thinkers, being plotted within the Ministry of Information. This opposition had resulted in their resignation from the Ministry. As a result, Hajjarian and others in his position were especially respected. Hidden forces and groups, like student groups that had been influenced by the alternative religious interpretations provided by Dr. Soroush, had become active and had entered the scene as reformists.

Likewise, secular writers whose lives continued to be in danger of assassinations by Information Ministry officials and agents of Hashemi Rafsanjani's government, both inside and outside of Iran, were prepared to lend their energy and support to the reformist movement, should an opening present itself. Women and youth, of all social classes, had reached their boiling point under the continuous pressure and intrusive behavior of agents who, with the excuse of safeguarding morality, would harass and arrest the public, particularly women and youth. The most basic demand of this sector was simply to have a little social freedom.

The majority of the people, despite their growing dissatisfaction, realized that they could not topple the regime, but they were fully willing to join a peaceful movement to create change, with the condition that they would not be expected to pay a high price for their support. The opposition forces within the government, which had access to information about the growing level of dissatisfaction among the Iranian population, were able to introduce an alternative candidate in the seventh round of presidential elections. He was a pleasant cleric with a different sort of look. He had a reputation for being a progressive thinker and was well regarded. He had been able to institute many reforms in the cultural sector through previous positions within the government. He was a member of the leftist clerics (*Ruhaniyun-e Mobarez*). His name was Mohammad Khatami. The opposition groups within the government were successful in ensuring that the candidacy of Mohammad Khatami, a moderate reform-minded cleric, was approved.

25

Khatami's election slogans were new and attractive. It was exactly what people had wished for and it was why they had supported the Islamic Revolution in 1979. He spoke of the rule of law. He valued political freedoms. He emphasized the rights of the opposition, and claimed that Iran was for all Iranians. His soft words impacted, more than any group, women and youth, who had become increasingly frustrated due to social pressures and limits. They felt compelled to vote for Khatami. He recognized the importance of creating and fostering the development of a vibrant civil society, which could become the foundation for a movement to achieve democracy. Limiting the intrusion into people's private lives, another of his slogans, could serve as an entry point for adopting and adhering to human rights standards. It had been many years since people were influenced by exciting political slogans. But Khatami's slogans brought new life to the people. The monthly *Adineh* ran a special issue in the spring of 1997 marking the Iranian New Year, which was focused on the following question: "If you were elected as the president, what would you do?"

Adineh also asked me this same question. At the time that *Adineh* put this question out there in an effort to solicit ideas, Faraj Sarkouhi, the editor, had disappeared. He was one of the main figures behind the process to collect signatures on "Letter 134" and one the six guests at the home of the German cultural attaché. The guests had spent that entire night being interrogated and threatened while blindfolded by intelligence agents at an unknown location. After that dinner party in 1996, Faraj was abducted from the transit area of Mehrabad Airport, while on his way to Germany. Under threats and torture, they had forced Faraj to write an incriminatory letter against himself and other members of the Iranian Writers' Society. In a very brave move,

Faraj had exposed the torture he had been subjected to through a letter he wrote, which was published outside the country. Now that Iran had moved toward electing a reformist president, Faraj Sarkouhi was under an extremely dangerous and difficult situation, imprisoned in an unknown location. Despite the fact that, as the editor of the first intellectual and forward thinking publication in the Islamic Revolution, he had played an important role in impacting the thinking of the time, he was not able to benefit from it, nor was he able to enjoy the fruits of his labor and sacrifices during the spring of 1997. His colleague, Parvin Ardalan, after a being arrested and detained for a time, was in hiding in rural areas and provinces of Iran. Nevertheless, *Adineh* was being managed based on Faraj's liking and direction, and continued to address issues in a manner that contributed significantly to the thinking of the intellectual community.

I was not able to respond to the question put forth by *Adineh* without consulting the constitution of the Islamic Republic. To be president in Iran, I would be required to work within the legal structures provided by the Iranian constitution. As a lawyer, too, I was required to defend my clients within this same framework.

For the first time, I began a process of examining the Islamic Constitution with a view toward understanding its capacity to implement the promises and slogans of reformists. Before this, I had always viewed and examined the constitution from the perspective of women's rights. But, from 1997, I began to examine the constitution in comparison to the legal standards that work to ensure democracy. Very quickly, I found that wanting does not necessary result in accomplishments.

Within the legal framework of the constitution, the president of Iran would not be able to live up to reformist promises and slogans and implement them. I found the constitution filled with obstacles. How could a reformist president come to terms with and bypass these obstacles? I developed a reply according to these findings and shared it with the Iranian people in an article I wrote for *Adineh*. In this article, I emphasized the fact that within the legal framework provided by the constitution, the president would not be able to live up to his vows and would not be able to defend the rights of the people.

26

Mohammad Khatami was elected president of Iran with over 20 million votes on May 23, 1997. Independent political parties and organizations did not exist in Iran. Nearly two decades after the revolution, the Iranian people joined together in a spontaneous manner and by merely exercising their right to vote, they elected Mohammad Khatami as their president. Khatami was elected on a platform promising the "rule of law," "protection for the rights of opposing groups," "civil society," "women's rights," "protection of the private sphere," and "freedom of speech." Everyone in my family, except for Azadeh, who was too young to vote, voted for Mr. Khatami, the reformist candidate. This was the first time since the inception of the Islamic Republic that we had exercised our right to vote. In this participation we were not alone. Many other Iranians, too, were voting for the first time since the revolution.

May 23, 1997 remains a memorable political day in the minds of the Iranian people. On that day, people restored their relationship with their government, which had been frozen since the early violent days of the revolution. The Iranian people imagined that Khatami not only wanted to, but also was able to act upon all that he had promised. Perhaps Khatami, too, believed that with the support of the people and their unprecedented vote of confidence, he could bring in line the Islamic Republic and the power structure with the demands of the people. In line with the constitution, Mohammad Khatami pledged to defend the rights of the people.

Iranians, as they did several other times in the past, such as during the Constitutional Revolution in 1906, decorated the streets in celebration of Khatami's victory. They rejoiced and turned their gaze toward the reformist president.

A few years later in 2001, when her father was abducted and imprisoned with no accountability from the government, my daughter Azadeh, who was only 12 years old in 1997, wrote a letter to President Khatami, asking him to investigate the case of her father. In this letter she described the sense of elation felt by the Iranian people on May 23, 1997, upon the election of a reformist president:

> Don't tell me about his room; he is in a solitary cell."
> Once again he was freed—a thin, tired, quiet man. Once a vibrant, gregarious talker, he had turned into a passive and indifferent listener.
>
> I was 15 when my mother, Mehrangiz Kar, a lawyer and a women's rights activist, was imprisoned. A few months earlier, my sister, Lily, had hurriedly left the country, leaving all her hopes and dreams in Iran. Government agents, or those who pretended to be government agents, had driven sleep from her eyes and peace from her heart.
>
> So it was that my father Dear Mr. President:
>
> I am a 17-year-old Iranian girl. My introduction to politics came through hearing your televised campaign interview when I was 12. On Election Day, I accompanied my parents to vote. Full of hope and great expectations, we drove across town while my father told us stories about the past and my mother looked at the gathering crowds in the street with her writer's eye. My sister boasted that she was old enough to vote, and I felt like becoming a political activist, but had to struggle with my birth date.
>
> When I was a year old, my father was imprisoned for the first time. He was not a thief, he was not a smuggler, he had committed no crime. Like so many other law-abiding Iranians, he became a prisoner who had no idea why he was in prison.
>
> When I was 6, he was hauled off to prison a second time. I remember banging my white shoes against the wall and shouting, "Don't tell me my father is traveling. His is in Evin Prisonand I were left alone to keep each other company. Family and friends spoke of me as a strong young woman. Only the walls in my room shared my fear and

frustration as I sobbed uncontrollably and banged them with my fists.

When my mother was finally released, I still wanted to see your smiling face and hear your words on government television, Mr. President – no matter that it was the same government television that had so recklessly distorted my mother's statements and slandered and insulted her.

Not long after she had secured her release from prison by posting backbreaking bail, my mother was diagnosed with cancer. I was 16 and could hardly wait now that I could vote for your election to a second term. Casting a ballot for the first time in my life was a thrill. I carefully wrote, "Seyed Mohammad Khatami," and became an adult. I am now accompanying my mother, who has traveled abroad to seek treatment for her illness.

A month ago we heard the news of my father's disappearance. Mr. President, my father, Siamak Pourzand, born November 24, 1931, was taken by unknown agents as he was seeing off some guests at his sister's house. He has not been heard from since. The last time my mother and I spoke with him, he told us that he was being followed by men on motorcycles and that he was in danger. We hadn't known what to do to help, and feel helpless now.

My mother sits in a corner quietly and waits for the phone to ring. I know well that a cancer patient has no hope of survival if she is tense and agitated. I don't know what to do for either of my parents.

This morning I woke up terrified. I had dreamed that an interrogator had slashed my father's neck, and I was running around hysterically trying to find a way to keep him alive. He called me back to him, saying, "It is no use, stay with me for a few more moments."

The road to Evin Prison has a sharp turn called "the repentance curve." If I ever pass that road, I will repent crimes that I have not committed so that I will not be taken in innocent and come out guilty. My only request of you, Mr. President, and fortunately you are still president, is to make an inquiry about my 70-year-old father's physical and psychological health and let me know how he is and where he is being held. I impatiently await a reply from your office.

Respectfully,

Azadeh Pourzand
First-time voter

27

After the May 23, 1997 elections, life in Iran gradually changed. Reform was offered through the newspaper stands. Two powerful ministers, appointed by Khatami to the Ministry of Culture and Islamic Guidance and the Ministry of Interior, were like rain in the dry deserts of Iran. These ministers allowed for consistent issuance of permits for books, magazines, newspapers and other publications. Organizations and associations were registered. The reformist press opened up key issues for discussion. For the first time in the modern history of Iran, discussions about the rights of the accused were expanded. This was a topic that had been forbidden in all of Iran's modern history, whether under the Islamic Republic, the rule of the Pahlavi dynasty, and even while Davar served as minister of justice during the time of Reza Shah. Under the ruling regimes, the accused, especially those accused of political or press crimes, never enjoyed any rights. Starting from 1997, we all worked together to analyze the existing laws, and where we found a positive point in support of the rights of those accused of political or press crimes, we would use the reformist press as podiums for advertising these rights.

The judiciary, almost immediately after the election of Mohammad Khatami, came under attack by the reformist press. Rightly, people had come to understand that the judiciary was the center of corruption. But few paid attention to the reasons for this corruption, which was rooted in the constitution. The judiciary, because of the constitution, cannot be an independent body and rather is controlled by the office of the Supreme Leader. How could a judiciary such as this, which does not enjoy independence, defend the rights of those who criticize the system and the Office of the Supreme Leader. The head of the judiciary is appointed by the Supreme Leader. All judges are appointed by the head of the judiciary, who can unseat them or transfer their posts. As such, an independent judiciary and unbiased judges within this system are only a dream.

Discussions demanding freedom and human rights, despite legal obstacles, had overtaken Iran. All that could be heard in Iran at that time were discussions about people's rights and citizen's rights. The constitution was interpreted in such as way as to give the impression that it was in line with democracy and human rights standards. Had the political power players connected with the Office of the Supreme Leader, who has absolute and ultimate control in Iran, joined the reformist movement, we could have turned Iran into a heaven. But this wish, while not childish, was also not rational or logical. There exist no examples of absolute powers, supported through the constitution, legal structures, economic structures and the armed forces, that have yielded easily to the demands and the will of the people.

Under the protection of reform, writers and intellectuals became accustomed to the sweet feeling of security. Faraj Sarkouhi was freed and interviews with him were published in the reformist press. His freedom demonstrated that the reformist government valued freedom of speech—at least at a level that could be easily witnessed. But the reformist honeymoon was short-lived. Those opposed to reform, who were at first shocked, slowly gathered strength and began a plan designed to crack down against reform. A few journalists working with the reformist press were arrested, and then released. The Fifth Parliament began the process of impeaching two powerful ministers appointed by Khatami. The Minister of Culture and Islamic Guidance received a vote of confidence, but the Minister of the Interior received a vote of no confidence and was ousted.

Reformist groups and groups opposing reforms began to organize, though in different camps. Groups opposed to reform began organizing and supporting their own pressure groups. They were responsible for disrupting gatherings. Students and student associations began organizing as well. The reformist government did not have the support of a political party or a well-developed political plan. This government relied on two forces—the student organizations and the press—for support and gave them much credit. Khatami failed to support and defend these two sectors when they came under severe attack by the conservative forces opposed to reform. In 1998 at the Islamic

Conference, which took place in Tehran, with the pretense of entering Islamic issues, Khatami announced that his interpretation of civil society was the same as Madinat ol Nabi, which in Islam is the source of charity and good fortune for Muslims. In other words, at this point, the president was claiming that by civil society he meant a religious society, which in essence was a contradiction to the modern idea of civil society and the plurality it sought to achieve. This claim by Khatami created a shock among his supporters, the first of a series to follow.

What happened during the organizing stage of the reformist activists did not mean that the "Orfigarayan," supporters of the separation of religion from the state, were also allowed to organize a group. Reformers had a religious base and they were supporting the framework of the Islamic Republic. So the supporters of separation of religion from the state, if they would make their opinions public, would not have been given a license for publishing papers or to register an organization or a party. In spite of this, the supporters of separation participated both in voting for Khatami and, after he was elected, offering their expertise to the reformist press. They saw reform as a step toward separation of religion from the state.

28

Ayatollah Yazdi, the head of the judiciary, quickly stole Khatami's slogan of "rule of law" and turned it into a weapon against reform. He and others opposed to reform fully understood that the legal structure of the country, and *sharia* law, were indeed limiting enough that by relying on the letter of the law, they could successfully destroy the reformist movement. Relying on the law, they focused their attacks against the press. This tactic allowed for the attacks to be viewed as legal. They appointed a young man, who had attended law school, as judge in one of the public courts. Saeed Mortazavi later became head of the Tehran Prosecutor's Office and tried to put a legal face to attacks against free speech. For years he headed the press court. He assembled a press jury, as a press regulatory body, with ties to conservative ruling groups opposed to reform. The jury did not represent the people. Rather it represented the government's ruling classes. The press laws were so biased against journalists, freedom of the press and freedom of speech that there was no room for maneuvering or putting forth legal interpretations in support of those accused under this law.

An extremely tragic development quickly overshadowed the news and reports from the press court. Dariush and Parvaneh Forouhar, two critics of the regime, were stabbed to pieces in their homes, and within a few days, two secular writers who were members of the Iranian Writers' Society, and who had an effective role in writing and publishing Letter No. 134, were abducted and strangled, their bodies abandoned in remote locations.

These four murders brought fear back to our homes. We were frightened of our own shadows. Lists were constantly published naming future targets for murder. The lists were precise in their information about those named, their locations, addresses, etc.

These lists included my name and the names of several members of the Iranian Writers' Society.

All of us were in search of a bit of security, which would not render itself easily. Like members of a family who sense fear and insecurity, some of the members of the Iranian Writers' Society who had chosen to remain in the country would regularly gather together. This group, with the support of a letter they managed to receive from the minister of culture and Islamic guidance, Ataollah Mohajerani, finally managed to hold a special emergency meeting of the members of the society.

The meeting was held at the home of Simin Behbehani, a brave poetess and activist. Twice, the emergency meeting was interrupted and attacked with the hopes to prevent voting by the members. Houshang Golshiri, a novelist, Changiz Pahlevan, a researcher, and Kazem Kardavani, a writer and professor, were able to intervene by showing the letter from the minister of culture, which allowed the Society to hold a public meeting of its membership. The meeting ended quickly with a sense of fear enveloping the occasion. But, the members did manage to elect a temporary secretariat for the Society.

Simin Behbehani, Shahla Lahiji, Shirin Ebadi and I were elected as members of the secretariat. The secretariat was charged with developing guidelines for the election of a permanent secretariat within a year's time. With the election of four women to the temporary secretariat, it was clear that the members of the Society had recognized that four women active in different areas—law, literature and culture—had worked bravely since the end of the eight-year war with Iraq, and were in a good position to lead the Society in its efforts to take advantage of the opportunities provided through the reform effort.

29

The murders of four secular intellectuals, carried out by agents of the Ministry of Intelligence (a fact that was divulged later), attracted the sympathy of religious intellectuals involved in the reformist government. Some well-known religious intellectuals paid their respects to secular mourners. Akbar Ganji was one of these individuals. The continuation of the reformist agenda, it was felt, would bring these two groups closer together. Both of these sectors were indeed in dire need of ensuring their security. The intelligence agents responsible for the murder of secular intellectuals had earlier claimed victims from among the religious intellectuals as well. Thus, the attraction of the two sectors toward cooperating, in an effort to combat the murderous forces that had found their way into the political regime, could serve as a generally positive development among intellectual circles in Iran, and connect these two circles of thinkers together.

Religious intellectuals and activists had taken on the editorial task of publishing reformist papers. These dailies, in fact, served as the platform for these groups and were dedicated solely to the message of religious intellectuals. Nevertheless, the reformist press took on the task of investigating the serial murders and provided secular intellectuals the opportunity to express their viewpoints within the reformist press. The Ministry of Culture and Islamic Guidance, now under the control of the reformist President Khatami, welcomed the possibility of a coalition between secular and religious intellectuals, which was until that point an unprecedented development. Each group, based on the information they had managed to obtain in the years leading up to the reform period, began exposing the behind-the-scenes developments that had led to the serial murders. The result of this effort has been documented in the reformist press.

Akbar Ganji, a journalist, and Nasser Zarafshan, a lawyer, took the greatest risks in the press battle with Intelligence Ministry agents who had committed kidnappings and murders before the reform period. The unspoken coalition between secular and religious thinkers seeking to weaken the strongholds of violence within the system quickly transformed into a revolution within the ruling circles. Ebrahim Nabavi, the skilled political satirist, played a critical role in speeding up these developments. Through the use of satire, he was able to inform the public about the strategies used for marginalizing and eliminating opposition intellectuals from the political and cultural scenes.

Shirin Ebadi, one of the lawyers representing the families of victims murdered through this plot, because of pressure from the security agents, was unable to demand and ensure justice for the families she represented. Other lawyers representing these families too were unsuccessful in their efforts. They could, with the support of Khatami's government and the reformist press, only expose the truth. These lawyers were either not accepted by the judiciary as representatives of the families, or when they were allowed to take on cases, they were given access to incomplete files, which were often missing vital information relevant to the cases they represented. While, for several years, writers and lawyers continued discussions on the issue of murder of intellectuals, demanding accountability, the judiciary staged trials and declared the cases resolved. The agents involved in the murders were able to maintain their positions without even being questioned or interrogated. Instead, all those involved in uncovering the cases and exposing those responsible for carrying out the murders were arrested, tried and sentenced to heavy prison terms. Some fled the country in fear for their lives. Those opposed to reforms were extremely fearful of a coalition between secular and religious intellectuals and activists.

In this dangerous period, I used my pen, as I always had, to question the structure and foundation of the laws of the Islamic Republic. In deciphering the reasons behind the serial murder of intellectuals, which according to some accounts had managed to eliminate 80 persons, I reached the conclusion that both the agents within the ministries as well as the Islamic Penal Code were to blame. The religious term *mahdur ol-dam* had entered the Islamic Penal Code and permitted murderers within the ruling classes the right to physically eliminate opponents of the regime. I had witnessed personally how the Islamic Penal Code had provided amnesty for those who had committed murder in the name of safeguarding the honor of their families. Now some of the judges overseeing the serial murder cases would openly provide reminders that if those committing murders believed the victims to be *mahdur ol-dam*, they would be subject to impunity. These judges would go on to explain that if the accused was not able to prove that the murder victim was indeed a *mahdur ol-dam*, then the murderer would be subject to paying blood money for the deceased, but would not be subject to *qesas*. Should the murderer be unable to pay the blood money imposed by the courts, the judges would explain, the state must take up the responsibility of paying the blood money to the family of the victim.

Entry into this religious discussion, criticism and examination of the politics of murder within the system of the Islamic Republic would indeed take away the feeling of security for all those who dared to take up the subject. Still, given the fact that the reformist press had provided an opportunity to expose the laws and practices that undermined human rights concepts, several lawyers chose to expose problems. They used this opportunity for promoting the concept and encouraging a discourse on human rights within Iran. Before the emergence of the reformist press, through the writings of books and articles on human rights, Shirin Ebadi and I were active in this arena. Later, other lawyers, under the security provided by Khatami's government and the opportunities provided in the reformist press, joined our ranks in expanding the discourse on human rights, and specifically in examining the obstacles to political development within the legal system of the Islamic Republic. The discussion on the rights of the accused, which is a major issue with respect to moving away from dictatorships and moving toward democracy through the process of strengthening civil society, was expanded during the reformist period.

The Press Law, which was adopted in 1990, had many problems. This law allowed for some freedom of the press, but part of the law actually limited greatly the freedom of the press. Lawyers would use the positive aspects of this law to defend their clients accused of violating press freedoms. Judges, set on limiting press freedoms and shutting down reformist publications, would use the negative aspects of this law to their own advantage. The same was true with respect to other sectors, and the Majles (parliament), even with the majority being reformist, was unable to remove these obstacles in favor of the press and civil society. In fact, any effort on the part of the Majles to ease these restrictions would be faced with greater resistance on the part of the judiciary, and would push the judges to rely more strictly on the negative aspects of the law.

The judiciary, which is under the supervision of the Office of the Supreme Leader, began an extensive and well-planned crackdown on the reformist press, which had taken a stand against the serial murders. The press courts relied on the abundant laws within the Islamic Republic to carry out this plan. Mostly those working within the press were accused of blasphemy and were convicted and imprisoned as a result. The broad arrests and imprisonment of journalists and editors resulted for the first time in an open discussion on the subject of torture.

Additionally, the reformist press provided lawyers the opportunity to openly and directly discuss the rights of the politically accused. This development allowed these lawyers to inform the public about political developments since the revolution and the adoption of the Islamic Constitution. Using the platform of the press, these lawyers were able to point out to the public that political developments after the revolution, which had led in many cases to the torture of dissidents and of those who chose to object to the status quo, were not only in direct opposition to international human rights standards, but were in fact in direct violation of the Islamic Constitution itself, specifically Article 168. Emphasis on the inclusion of a jury in trials was indeed one of the requirements of the constitution that was never adhered to by the judicial system.

Widespread criticism of the government and ruling establishment through the platform of the print media – which had been forbidden and taboo during the Pahlavi era and in the years following the revolution and leading up to the reform period – had begun. Some of the better-known figures of the reform movement even extended this criticism to the Office of the Supreme Leader, asking the Assembly of Experts, charged with electing the Supreme Leader, to provide oversight on the conduct of the Supreme Leader and report their findings yearly to the people.

The Iranian public, which had during the Pahlavi era been denied the opportunity to criticize the system (except for very short-lived and eventful periods often interspersed with unrest), and which had become thirsty for any form of criticism of the system after the Islamic Revolution, welcomed the actions of the reformist press. The sales of the reformist print media quickly soared. The Iranian public would form daily lines at the news kiosks, in anticipation of the next additions of their favorite dailies.

For the reformist newspapers, the red line was drawn around the crimes committed in the first decade of the revolution. The reformist papers would not investigate or write about them. So many people inside and outside Iran became angry and unsatisfied. Despite this situation, the opposition of the reform within the Islamic Republic could not tolerate the reformist press.

Those opposed to reforms, who occupied the government institutions supervised by the Supreme Leader and who witnessed the enlivening political scene within the country, realized that while Khatami had the wide support of the people, they could not fully crack down on the reform movement. On the other hand, Khatami's minister of culture and Islamic guidance, who was in charge of the press and issued licenses for the establishment of new publications, had chosen a smart strategy for ensuring the survival of the reformist press. The minute the judiciary would shut down a daily, a license would be issued for the publication of another daily. So it was that when one daily closed down, another one would start up under a different name, fully committed to promoting reformist strategies. For example, the daily *Toos* was shut down, so then *Jame'h* took its place. When *Jame'h* was shut down, *Neshat* replaced it. For the first time in Iran, the game of politics, through a legal effort to come face to face with the establishment, had become exciting and attractive.

This game had a set of rules and the reformists continuously emphasized that these rules must be adhered to in efforts to challenge the anti-reform bodies within the government. They insisted that the game of politics must continue without violence. But those opposed to reform did not adhere to the same rules. Besides cracking down on the reformists through the press courts, the opponents of the reform movement organized "pressure groups" assigned with the duty of disrupting the gatherings of reformists. Through these means, those opposed to reform disrupted the rules of the game. The attacks carried out by these "pressure groups" gradually disrupted efforts of reformists to hold meetings. In fact, during one of these attacks, two key government ministers were beaten. Ataollah Mohajerani, the minister of culture and Islamic guidance, and Abdollah Nouri, the minister of interior, were attacked by pressure groups at a general meeting. These attacks were indeed a direct attack on Khatami's reform government. By providing press permits and registration permits for independent non-governmental organizations, these two ministers had worked to create a more open society within the framework of the Islamic Republic's constitution.

Other ministers of the Khatami government were not targeted by anti-reform forces as much as these two were. Khatami's government lacked a well-developed plan for promoting reforms, and the ministers within his government were largely following the plans that were already in existence and had been followed in the past. Contrary to his promises, Mohammad Khatami was not able to convince opponents of reform of the importance of including women in the cabinet as ministers. Instead, he appointed a woman as the head of the Center for Women's Participation, associated with the Office of the President, and he appointed one woman as a vice president to head the Organization for Environmental Protection. Discussions on women's rights were largely marginalized during Khatami's first term, 1997-2001. Overshadowed by discussions on the rights of the accused, the free press and political crimes, women's issues took a back seat.

Faezeh Hashemi, the daughter of former president Akbar Hashemi Rafsanjani, building on her father's power and in line with her own creativity and initiative, established *Zan (Woman)* daily. This was the first daily ever to be dedicated to women's issues in Iran. It was focused on improving the status of women, and worked to attract the support of Islamic scholars and *mojtaheds* active in alternative and forward-leaning interpretations of women's rights within Islam. This daily quickly received attention, but in the attacks against the press, it too was shut down in 1999. *Zan* daily published a special addition on the occasion of the Press Exhibit in 1999. The special addition included interviews with a number of leading activists engaged on women's behalf, including myself. Fundamentalists never forgave Faezeh for this brave effort.

At this Tehran Press Exhibit, I was present when, during Ms. Faezeh Hashemi's speech, the law enforcement forces stormed the *Zan* newspaper booth and ended the anti-censorship discussions. That day the *Zan* newspaper booth was full of people who were learning how to protect freedom of speech and press while keeping their peace and staying calm.

30

After 1997, the political role of Iranian youth in challenging the world in which they lived was crystallized more than it had ever been before. By utilizing a historic opportunity, university students began to wage a peaceful struggle in defense of reform. In their confrontation with the crises in the reform movement, these students demonstrated a remarkable level of maturity by refraining from violence and utilizing peaceful measures in their confrontation with forces that chose violence as their main strategy. The security and intelligence forces supporting conservative groups not only engaged a strategy of "women against women" in an effort to quash women's demands for their rights – a continuous strategy from the start of the revolution in 1979 – but also, with the excuse of a Cultural Revolution in 1980, put forth the strategy of "students against students" as a means to quell student and youth demands. In all the years leading up to the reform period, the universities remained under the control of intelligence forces. These intelligence forces, however, were guised under the cloak of university and student organizations.

Before the start of the reform period in 1997, independent organizations and political parties with the aim of criticizing the ruling elite and government had not been established. Intelligence forces would only allow those associated with the ruling elite, who maintained absolute control, to organize. Student organizations were marred with a heavy political feel and the discourse of human rights and democratization were conspicuously absent from these organizations.

The history of establishing student organizations within the framework of universities goes back to the years 1941-1951, and the nationalization of the oil industry under the leadership of Dr. Mohammad Mossadegh. During that time, a group of nationalists who also identified themselves as religious and who were opposed to the Shah, like Mehdi Bazargan and Yadollah Sahabi, took the lead in establishing Islamic organizations in some universities. These organizations, while emphasizing Islamic and national ideals, would in some instances act in opposition to Marxist groups, which were active within universities. Although these Islamic student organizations were independent, nevertheless, after the coup against Mossadegh in 1953, they too were dismantled.

After the victory of groups associated with Ayatollah Khomeini in September 1979 and the subsequent transfer of power, representatives from Islamic organizations within universities, which had come to life in the political aftermath of the revolution, visited with Khomeini and asked for his guidance. "Go on and consolidate unity," said Ayatollah Khomeini to the student representatives. After this visit, the Office for the Consolidation of Unity, with elected representatives from the various Islamic student organizations, was established.

The Office to Consolidate Unity (*Daftar-e Tahkim-e Vahdat*) at that point was influenced and controlled by a leftist Islamist ideology. Ayatollah Khomeini also represented this line of thinking, and the Office to Consolidate Unity (Daftar-e Tahkim-e Vahdat) took on the role of a pressure group in support of Khomeini and leftist Islamists. The leftist Islamists promoted extreme ideologies, such as war with the United States, government controlled economy, and severe crackdowns and elimination of opponents.

If we were to assess and evaluate the role of Islamic student organizations in the first decade following the revolution, with the criteria and values of today's Iran, we would find these organizations to have played a negative role in opposition to democratic movements and human rights standards. This role was especially negative with respect to educational value systems within the university setting. The Cultural Revolution, which resulted in the closure of universities, provided the student organizations with the opportunity to establish value-based selection processes within the university setting, which also undermined the concept of free elections in these organizations. These selection processes were established largely after the ouster of students and professors deemed out of step with the value system promoted by the revolution. The film *The Hidden*

Half, directed by Tahmineh Milani, provides an historical account of the developments in the university setting, where students filled with excitement and revolutionary fervor set out to systematically eliminate and exclude forces they deemed to be in opposition to their own thinking.

At the end of the eight-year war with Iraq, and with the emergence of Ayatollah Hashemi Rafsanjani as the president of Iran, limitations were placed on the activities and extremism promoted by the Islamic student organizations. The extreme position advocated by these student organizations was seen unfavorably by the Rafsanjani administration. He claimed that he wanted to promote privatization and social welfare. On the other hand, a new generation of students with differing perspectives had entered the university system. This new generation was younger and opposed the thinking of their predecessors, who had stormed the U.S. Embassy to take its staff hostage, who insisted on value-based selection systems within the university environment, a government-controlled economy and severe crackdowns on opposition groups. In other words, the entrance of a younger generation of students into the university system, in a time of peace, had constricted the space available to older students with revolutionary and extremist tendencies, who wanted to continue indefinitely to remain within the university organizations with the intent of preventing moderate policies.

Some university professors, who had managed and promoted the policies resulting from the Cultural Revolution, reconsidered their own extremist positions. It is accurate to claim that Dr. Mohammad Soroush was the bravest and most effective of the university professors who had, in line with the changing demands of Iranian society and the changing political and social climate, reconsidered his thinking. In the second decade following the revolution, Dr. Soroush began to defend the concept of separation of religion and state, and with the assistance of Akbar Ganji published a number of articles and books addressing this issue. The students entering university in the second decade following the revolution were greatly influenced by the thinking and the writing of Dr. Soroush. As a result, these students, even those attracted to a theocracy, turned their backs on the intellectual stalemate resulting from the Cultural Revolution.

So it was that during peacetime, through the influence of the younger generation that benefited from different characteristics and perspectives, the Islamic student organizations were transformed into bastions of democratic demands and thinking. With time, these student organizations were able to hold elections. Before this period, though, those at the helm of these organizations were vetted based on their belief systems and values. But in the year 1996, the elections within student organizations at most universities were freer than they had ever been before.

Despite the fact that before the start of the reform period in 1997 no independent organizations or political parties that advocated reforms existed, the student organizations, even in those difficult times, had begun the process of organizational growth. These organizations, with representatives in the Office to Consolidate Unity (*Daftar-e Tahkim-e Vahdat*), quickly lent their strength to the reform movement as thinkers and implementers, and in step with the press, began a discourse on human rights and democratization.

Still, student organizations with ties to fundamentalist groups remained undemocratic, and their members were appointed, not freely elected. To this day, these organizations remain institutions where ideological leanings play a significant role in devising their power structure. These fundamentalist organizations continue to receive financial support from conservative groups, and when necessary, they play the role of pressure groups and often work to disrupt the gatherings of more progressive student organizations. When Khatami was elected in 1997, the Office to Consolidate Unity (*Daftar-e Tahkim-e Vahdat*) published statements outlining its political leanings. Since then, Islamic organizations allied themselves with reformists, also referred to as the modern leftist Islamists. The leftist Islamists, who identified themselves as followers of Ayatollah Khomeini, were, after the start of the reform period, referred to as traditional leftists.

The thinking of the reformists, or modern leftists, did not include war with the United States, government control of the economy, or widespread crackdowns against opposition groups. Instead, this group emphasized a more moderate foreign policy, privatization of the economy, rule of law, strengthening of civil society, toleration of opposition, and efficiency in the elected branches of government. The most important characteristic of

Islamic student organizations after 1997 was their emphasis on free elections. With the exception of a few organizations, the members of these groups respect the results of their elections and allow those members who had been elected to serve on their governing boards, and to fulfill their terms of duty, irrespective of their political or ideological leanings. It is safe to say that these organizations, by valuing and choosing democratic processes, have reached a point where Islam no longer dictates their activities and leanings.

The Central Council of the Office to Consolidate Unity (*Daftar-e Tahkim-e Vahdat*) has been able to bring attention to important political developments since 1997. In the first few years of his presidency, this council was a staunch supporter of President Mohammad Khatami. Further, a human rights discourse and demand for freedoms, democracy and women's rights had entered the mandate of the council since 1995. Despite the fact that differences in opinion and beliefs do exist among council members, the Office to Consolidate Unity (*Daftar-e Tahkim-e Vahdat*) has moved toward a more secular approach. The developments around the student movement in 1999 sped the process of secularization for the Office to Consolidate Unity (*Daftar-e Tahkim-e Vahdat*). Their collective experiences proved to them that the mixing of religion and state would make it impossible to respect human rights and obtain democracy, and as a result, the reform movement would be faced with a dead end.

The declaration to "Bypass Khatami" in 2000 demonstrated another commitment on the part of the student movement toward separation of religion and state. This declaration was issued in response to an attempt by the Sixth Parliament, also known as the Reform Parliament, to reform and democratize the press laws. The effort was thwarted as a result of a letter written by the Supreme Leader asking the parliament to withdraw the initiative. The reaction of Khatami as president and Mehdi Karoubi as the head of the parliament was not as was expected, and they acquiesced to the demands of the Supreme Leader.

The letter that the Central Committee of the Office to Consolidate Unity (*Daftar-e Tahkim-e Vahdat*) wrote to Kofi Annan at the United Nations in 2003, which outlined the obstacles to democracy within the system of the Islamic Republic, also demonstrates the transition in thought of the members of the Islamic student organizations. The signing of the call for a referendum on the Constitution of the Islamic Republic, which was signed by several members of the Central Council of the Office to Consolidate Unity (*Daftar-e Tahkim-e Vahdat*) and a few human rights activists including Naser Zarafshan and me in 2005, demonstrates further the transition toward a more secular perspective within this organization. In this letter, the request is made for a referendum to take place in Iran under the supervision of international organs, and that people should be called to freely express their opinions about amending and rewriting the Constitution of Iran in accordance with the international human rights doctrine.

Further, the Office to Consolidate Unity (*Daftar-e Tahkim-e Vahdat*) has, since 1997, consistently provided space within the university setting and within its publications for human rights and women's rights activists to air their issues, and to express their ideas and demands with respect to equality of citizens. This was an unprecedented move and a golden opportunity for women's rights and human rights activists, from which I also benefited greatly.

31

A number of other activists and I were regularly invited by universities to speak about the legal obstacles to ensuring women's rights and human rights within the Islamic Republic. Likewise, nationalist-religious groups put women's rights and human rights at the center of their political agendas. During the years 1997-2000, I would appear regularly at university centers to discuss these issues. At the invitation of nationalist groups, I would also provide a critical analysis of the legal system, including the constitution. I was invited to these types of meetings not only in Tehran but also in the provinces and in cities like Mashad, Qazvin, Shiraz and Khomeini Shahr (Sedeh). These invitations by student organizations and women's organizations connected with reformist groups or nationalist groups, and their potential for informing the public, led me to believe that if the reform movement were to continue, it would eventually turn into a revolution that would destroy forever the historical roots of despotism in Iran. Leftist religious thought, influenced by the thinking of university students, was increasingly coming closer at its core to notions of separation of religion and state.

At universities, students associated with the ruling institutions, who believed that reform was undermining and destroying religious values, would question and interrogate me. They reminded me that all my criticisms of Islamic law were indeed an apparent indication of my opposition to Islam. This was the same perspective that, in the years prior to the reform period, the daily *Kayhan*, *Kayhan Air*, *Sobh* monthly and the Governmental Radio and Television Broadcast had promoted. But what was a new and interesting development was the direct confrontation of the two perspectives—reformists and conservatives—within political and university gatherings.

After the bloody crackdowns that were carried out in the first decade of the revolution, human rights and women's rights defenders could rarely utilize public and university meetings to criticize the situation in Iran. In fact, they were not allowed entry into these gatherings, and only the conservative and fundamentalist groups were provided with opportunities to speak. Now I had arrived upon a complicated and dangerous situation. In every meeting in which I participated, inevitably there would be statements against my husband and me, which would be distributed to participants. On occasion, I would be informed that after a meeting, those in charge of organizing the event would be brought in for interrogations.

One of these events took place in the city of Mashad. I was invited to give a on Women's Day by a group of Muslim women who observed the *hejab* by wearing the traditional black *chador* that attested to their piety. After the event, upon my return to Tehran, I learned that the manager of the organization that had sponsored the event had been put under extreme pressure by the information agents at the Astane Qods Razavi, the foundation charged with overseeing the finances and activities related to the shrine of Imam Reza, located in the city of Mashad. The manager had been put under such intense pressure that she suffered a heart attack and was transferred to the hospital as a result. Until then, I did had not realized that Ayatollah Tabassi, the head of the foundation, benefited from absolute power in Khorassan, the province in which his foundation was based. I also did not realize that he had at his disposal his own intelligence forces.

It was through the process of attending these types of events and speaking in public political and social forums that I became familiar with the complex network and structure of power and power relations within Iran. What gave me confidence, at least with respect to continuing these types of activities, was the realization that these power brokers, despite the monetary, intelligence and security resources at their disposal, were unable to prevent persons like myself from appearing on the scene. They would only create fear in the hearts of people like me in the hopes that we would vacate the political and social scene. This reality fully demonstrated that had the reform movement benefited from strong leadership, it would have been able to achieve and realize its own democratic and revolutionary ideals in a matter of a decade.

I don't deny, however, that at times I was frightened to no end, and every time I was harassed during or after a public appearance I would vow never to accept another invitation. Inevitably, I was unable to stay true to those vows. Each time, moved by my own heartfelt convictions and motivated by the desires of those very same people who would wait anxiously at newsstands in anticipation of reading news on yet another democratic development in their homeland, I would appear for another public meeting.

32

My diary reads:

I have been invited to the city of Sedeh, which is the birthplace of my ancestors. A student organization has taken on the task of inviting me to a meeting in honor of the birth of Fatemeh Zahra, the daughter of the prophet Mohammad. The auditorium is filled. I am fully aware of the historical and cultural importance of this city. The city is comprised of three villages and is within 10 kilometers of the historic city of Isfahan. Sedeh has recently been officially recognized as a city and is famous for its religious extremism. Both the Shah's regime and the government of the Islamic Republic had tried greatly, but unsuccessfully, to put an end to the custom of inflicting injury on one's body with a dagger as a mourning tradition within the 10 days of *Ashura*[1]. I remember well staring at and examining with great shock the marks of the dagger on my father's head, which resulted from his participation in the *Ashura* mourning festivities at the time of his youth. The people of Sedeh are also famous for the value they place on the honor of women. Before the revolution, they did not

---

[1] The practice of inflicting injury to one's body or, *qameh zani*, is a tradition observed by Shiite Muslims during the mourning rituals of *Ashura*—10 days marking the martyrdom of Hossein, the grandson of the Prophet Mohammad. During a particular hour on the day of *Ashura*, which is the anniversary of the martyrdom of Hossein, some mourners use the *qameh*, which is dagger of sorts, and drag it on their scalps, bloodying the mourning festivities and adding to the religious excitement and fervor of the event. Reza Shah Pahlavi was the first to fight this tradition and to try to prevent it. Several of the officials of the Islamic Republic too have tried to put an end to this bloody tradition. But in the city of Sedeh, mourners still use the *qameh* as part of their mourning festivities and traditions marking the death of Hossein.

allow their daughters the slightest of social freedoms. Before the revolution, and in honor of the Shah, the name of Sedeh was changed to Homayoun Shahr, with the aim of expressing the allegiance of the town to the monarchy. After the revolution, the name of the city was changed to Khomeini Shahr.

Now, at this place and time, I am witness to a historic development in the land of my ancestors. Before this meeting, I took the opportunity to visit the city of Sedeh a bit. I visited all those narrow streets, stories of which were told and retold to me as a child. In Sedeh, paved roads, modern buildings, high-rise apartments, coexist with dirt roads. The vast campus of the university, which to the residents of Sedeh is known as the best remembrance of the Shah's efforts on their behalf, is a source of great pride for the local community and lends to the city a level of credibility.

But, the real sign of modernity in the city of Sedeh is not the modern buildings or the paved roads; rather it is the girls and young women who daily make their way to school. These same girls, during the time of the Shah, could be seen with the thickest of coverings as their *chador*s, but now they are wearing scarves and manteaus. The supporters of anti-woman traditions have surprisingly abandoned their fight against this very apparent development in women's lives. These types of developments force me to gain distance from my exclusively intellectual perspective and to become familiar with all that is hidden within the various aspects of life in my country. Iran is not summarized in Tehran and developments in the capital city alone. I realize that forced *hejab*, which has created many problems for us, in places that are far away and hard to access, has acted as a force against itself. This development has helped me distance myself from the world of "musts" and "must nots," from a black and white view of issues, and from absolutes. My mother used to say that the *chador* (extreme Islamic veil) of the women of Sedeh is like the cover of night, thick and dark and wrapped around women in a confining fashion. Now, except for a few elderly women, the rest of the women don't wear this type of *chador*. Not only do they not wear this type of *chador*, but rarely can you spot a woman in Sedeh wearing a *chador* at all. Instead, they wear overcoats, trousers and headscarves or habits.

A deep transformation has taken place, impacting social norms, which the men in Sedeh have not been able to prevent. The great patriarch, Khomeini, by relying on his absolute power derived from *sharia*, has proclaimed that a manteau, scarf or habit for head covering does in fact constitute proper *hejab*. The men of Sedeh have been forced to retreat in the face of the absolute power of Khomeini in this arena, and accept this new form of the *hejab* for their daughters. I see a chorus made up of young school girls dressed in light blue uniforms who, accompanied by a group of male musicians, are singing an anthem in celebration of Women's Day. The organizers of these festivities fear the repercussions of their own work and claim that this is the first time that young girls have appeared in public with colored *hejab*. They explain that they have acquired written permission letters from each of the girls' fathers in advance of the event, and still they are fearful of the reactions of the fundamentalist elements in the city. The girls sing the anthem with confidence.

I can't believe that the presence of such a small group can so quickly turn into an important social development attracting such widespread attention that promises the possibility of negative retaliation. I sit behind the microphone. I criticize the Islamic laws and their implementation and point to the fact that it is important and beneficial to offer new interpretations of religion, so that women are able to participate in all facets of social and political life. At the end of my speech, the same old accusations are launched against me. For example, one person asks, "How come your claim comes in contradiction to Imam Ali's recommendation not to consult women?" It seems that the opponents to reform and freedom always use the words of the prophet and Imams when they are faced with challenges to which they cannot respond. Finally, my speech comes to an end. I am relieved that I have put behind me another possible dangerous situation. I walk toward the exit when suddenly a group intercepts my path and surrounds me, preventing me from leaving the auditorium.

I quickly find one of my relatives who has attended the meeting and toss him my handbag. I feel threatened. This wall of flesh has quickly surrounded me. Men who believe that unrelated men and women cannot come into physical contact with one another have encircled me. There is no way for me to escape. There is video camera hanging over my head the cameraman has gone on stage in an effort to capture on film all that is taking place. I come to believe this is the end for me, but it seems that those who have surrounded me do not intend to physically assault me; rather they are continuously and in a loud voice asking me the same question over and over again:

"If you are telling the truth, then explain to us, make us understand, why is it that God has never chosen a woman as his messenger or prophet? Why is it that from among 124,000 messengers of God, not even one of them is a woman?"

Faced with the questions of these angry young men, who claim to be members of the Islamic Organization of the University of Isfahan, I hear reflections of the voice of my grandmother, Bibi. It seems that the beliefs of Bibi, a woman who was born over a century ago, have somehow come to occupy the minds of the young people living in the year 2000. These young people have lent their anti-woman beliefs to the ruling classes. It is as if their beliefs are tools in the hands of our rulers, which are used against women. I don't believe that the Islamic government has played a significant role in infusing the minds of these young people with negative ideas about the role of women. Rather I believe that they derive their beliefs from their mothers, who have influenced their view of the world with anti-woman sentiments and ideals.

As I am about to suffocate from the smell of sweat exuded from the wall of flesh that surrounds me, a hand breaks up the crowd and searches for and grabs my hand and pulls me away. The force of the pull of this hand is so great that I fear my arm will dislodge from my shoulder. The strong young man has sensed the terror and pulls me with him, ignoring the roar of the crowd that has surrounded me. According to a plan devised in advance of the event, we exit the auditorium from a hidden door. The young man leading me out locks the door behind us. We both run away from the building. There is a taxi waiting for us.

33

I quickly learned that the young man who had rescued me was one of the many young students who had reached adulthood after the revolution and at a time of political upheavals. He was intent on expanding the atmosphere of dialogue within his hometown of Sedeh. In the last hours of my trip to Sedeh, I had a chance to better acquaint myself with this young man, who had in fact saved my life. He, too, wanted to talk.

He claimed that he loved his mother dearly, but he could not share with her his serious problems. He believed that his mother had a closed mind. In explanation, he said that he had met a young female student and would like to marry her. But his mother did not approve of the girl and was opposed to their marriage. In her view, a girl who befriends men was not acceptable. The young man felt extremely lonely and without even realizing it, he blurted out, "I wish you were my mother."

I tried hard not to cry. I lowered my gaze so that he could not see the tears in my eyes, and I said, "From now on, you can believe that I am your mother."

This time his eyes filled with tears and he explained with regret: "But you can't go with me in my mother's place to ask for this girl's hand in marriage."

He was right and we both laughed out loud. The young man continued: "But you can telephone her father on my behalf. Everyone knows that your ancestors were from Sedeh. He will accept your word."

I hesitated for an instant, as I was afraid of entering this realm. "How can I be helpful?" I inquired.

The young man gave me the telephone number for the father's place of employment. I contacted him. The girl's father was very cordial and polite. He listened to my words, but his reply to my request was negative. He explained: "I will not allow my daughter to marry into this family. This young man's mother is backward thinking and too zealous in her religious beliefs. My daughter has a university education. I am afraid that she may have a difficult time in this family."

At the insistence of the young man, I called the girl's father several times, but my attempts were not fruitful.

I have many political memories from my trip to Sedeh, but this one memory tends to resonate with me and I left with the daunting question of how it was possible to be a woman and to still promote anti-woman sentiments, and to oppose women's demands.

A few years later, in 2004, when a majority of conservative fundamentalists were elected to the Iranian Parliament, I heard on several occasions the female members of the parliament make statements that were in direct contradiction to women's demands and women's progress. These statements included:

"Polygamy has many benefits for women and we must re-move the obstacles faced by men in acquiring several wives"; and, "In efforts to resolve the problems of prostitution, we should immediately execute 10 prostitutes in public, so as to prevent other women from prostituting themselves."

34

Islamic moral codes, which the founders of the Islamic Republic claimed to be protecting, were instituted at the start of the revolution. These codes changed the personal and social norms of society. Forced *hejab* and storming of recreational facilities, such as swimming pools, exercise facilities and ski resorts, where people of both sexes commingled, are examples of the Islamic programs that extremist groups implemented in the name of Islam after the victory of the Islamic Revolution. By emphasizing that Islamic revolutionaries had come to destroy the roots of moral corruption, these extremists also set fire to an area in Tehran called Shahre No, which was a legal prostitution center in operation under the supervision of the Health Ministry during the time of the Shah. After the burning of Shahre No (meaning New Town), famous prostitutes were executed and stoned to death in both Tehran and the provinces in line with Islamic doctrine.

With the establishment of the Islamic Republic in 1979 and with the passing of the Islamic Penal Code, which included a variety of violent punishments, all of these violent revolutionary acts took on a legal form. This atmosphere familiarized the Iranian population with a constant state of fear and terror. Up until the revolution, only those individuals who would dissent from the political status quo under the rule of the Shah would become fearful for their own safety. After the revolution, personal behavior and private matters, if they clashed with the values announced by the state, were defined as crimes that could be punishable by both imprisonment, flogging and fine.

The institution of Islamic moral codes at first glance sought to cleanse society, but with time, the implementers and supporters of these types of programs actually began to contradict their own moral codes at the personal and social levels. Lawyers would witness that some court cases indicated the support and involvement of government officials in the creation of prostitution rings, distribution of illegal drugs, trafficking of women, and the creation of corruption rings. These lawyers came to believe that lower socioeconomic classes had indeed suffered and been taken advantage of as a result of the revolution more so than other groups.

In my professional life, two figures, Haji Organi—someone who worked for one of the government organs—and Mama Pari, are of special importance. These two, who had established a trafficking ring that would lure young women and force them into prostitution, provided information about the involvement of some government officials in corruption rings of this kind. In other words, some the same people who under pretense of Islam and religion would arrest citizens and flog and imprison them would misuse their governmental powers and positions, to recreate Shahre No in the form of homes, which appeared to be the residences of middle- and lower-income families.

These prostitution houses benefited from a level of immunity and security, as each one was protected by a person working within the morality committees, police forces or revolutionary organizations. These officials did not benefit monetarily from the proceeds brought in by the prostitutes, but in exchange for their protection they would receive free services and would freely enter and leave the homes. Mama Pari owned one of these prostitution homes in Tehran. She had unexpectedly been turned in by one of her co-workers and was subsequently arrested and imprisoned. She asked me to serve as her defense lawyer. It took several months before the courts allowed me access to the case file. To my surprise, the judge in charge of the case on several occasions prevented me from taking on Mama Pari's case. I could not understand why he did not want me to take on a case that was not classified as being political. The judge was a cleric with a turban, and every time he would see me pursuing this particular case, he would sit me down and have a talk with me. He would insist that it was not "appropriate" for a respectable woman like me to take on such cases; that I was too good to be dealing with cases of prostitution.

I resisted these advice sessions and with my continued insistence I was able to make the judge understand that as a lawyer and according to the law, I had the right to represent and defend

Mama Pari against the crimes with which she was charged. I also used a few of my own tricks to combat the runaround I was getting from the judge. I explained to him that should I not be allowed to represent Mama Pari, she may be forced to hire a male lawyer, who could take on the case. With this explanation, the judge surrendered.

"You mean that this corrupt woman wants to get a lawyer to represent her at all costs. Even a male lawyer?" the judge asked.

I explained: "Yes, the defendant has given me until tomorrow to reach an agreement with you on this case, and be allowed to represent her in court. Otherwise, tomorrow one of my male colleagues will be here as her defender."

The judge adjusted his turban. He ordered his secretary to bring me the case file. He also ordered me to read through the file in his presence. He emphasized that I did not have the right to request a photocopy of the case file. Requesting and receiving a photocopy of the case file of the client is one of the basic rights of legal defenders within all judicial systems. But, in the judicial system of Iran, lawyers were often denied access to case files in this manner, according to the likes and dislikes and personal styles of judges.

The secretary brought me the case file. The file was so thick that it frightened me. How was I able to make sense of the case in such a short time? Without objecting, I sat in a corner and opened the file and started reading. The judge continued with his work.

Who was Mama Pari? She was the mother of a martyred soldier. She was young and beautiful. She had lost her only male child in the Iran-Iraq War and lived with a few of her daughters. She did not have a husband. The girls were orphans and after the death of their brother, according to them, they did not have a caregiver or breadwinner.

Mama Pari had developed a relationship with revolutionary organizations that provided assistance to families of martyrs. But the assistance provided by these organizations was not enough to cover her expenses. She had met a man who held an important post within one of the revolutionary organizations. Everyone called him Haji Organi. He had developed an affection for Mama Pari and enjoyed their visits. The visits increased.

One day, Haji Organi said to Pari: "Why do you keep going from office to office to make ends meet? You should start your own business. I will help you."

"How can I start a business with no money and no support?" Pari asked Organi.

Haji Organi had advised Pari and told her that she could start a business in her home. He had explained that she could find young girls on the street who were looking for some food and shelter.

"There are plenty of takers," he explained. "I will tell the guys (meaning the morality police) not to bother you. But you should be careful. Don't recruit married women. That will cause you problems. The customers can enter into a temporary marriage contract with the girls (or *sigheh*) and this way you won't have problems with respect to abiding by *sharia* law."

With the guidance of Haji Organi, Pari, my client, who was the mother of a martyred son and several teenage daughters, was transformed into Mama Pari. In Iranian culture and Persian literature, women who managed prostitution houses were either referred to as Mama (meaning mother) or Madam. Pari had become widely known as Mama Pari. In the case against her, the courts and officials had tried as much as they could to minimize the role and presence of Haji Organi, who was an official responsible for providing assistance to the families of martyrs. Mama Pari was in prison, but Haji Organi and the officials connected with him, who protected Mama Pari and were her regular customers, remained free and on the streets. At best, they had been brought in for questioning as witnesses, but returned to their work and offices.

Haji Organi had advised Pari to be patient. He had promised that he would make arrangements for her release. While defending Pari, I came to realize that operators of prostitution rings usually start their businesses with the support of groups within the government. I also realized that the time these people spend in prison ends up being productive and lucrative for them. Mama Pari confided in me that Madams, while in prison, use their time to identify and target young beautiful girls who have been arrested by the morality police for fraternizing with the opposite sex, having free sexual relations with men or going to mixed gender parties, and recruit them as prostitutes. They give these young girls numbers through which they can contact them upon their release. When released from prison, many of these girls are shunned by their families and when faced with nowhere to go, they contact the Madams out of desperation. The women's prisons in the Islamic Republic, as a result, have turned into recruiting grounds for prostitution rings. The ever-increasing statistics on prostitution in Iran are a testament to the poor economic conditions of women, the infiltration of prostitution ringleaders into prisons and the supporting role of some officials within the government, who promote these establishments.

Mama Pari and Haji Organi played an important role in my professional life. Studying this case exposed the realities of prostitution and corruption for me. As a result, I began to distrust and question the forces and officials in the Islamic Republic who at least appeared to promote and protect Islamic values and morals. Mama Pari was both young and beautiful and a willing participant in this scheme. Extreme poverty and need forced others to fall into this profession and the evil hands of people like Haji Organi. For example, I once represented an old woman who was not only extremely poor, but also conservative and cautious. She had been charged with running a prostitution house, and as a result had been sentenced to 10 years in prison, due to serve her term in a distant location known for its difficult climate. The old imprisoned woman, who was crying up a storm, explained that she had only one son, who had died in the war. After the death of her son, she lived in a small two-room house and received assistance from the Martyrs Foundation.

She was a simple woman and tended to trust and listen to those who seemed to be religious and devout. She explained that the officials had taken note of her difficult living situation and wanted to help her financially. She intended to help her nieces and nephews with the extra income. Her sister had lost her husband and her children had lost their father and did not have a breadwinner in the family. According to the old woman, the officials had suggested that she move to one of the rooms in her home and leave the other unused. They suggested that she furnish the room with a bed and rent it out to members of the morality police and their families who traveled to Tehran from the provinces, so that they would not need to stay in hotels. The visitors would stay one or several nights. In return, some of the officials of the Morality Police would provide her with financial assistance. The old woman explained that on occasion a man and woman, whom she believed to be a married couple, would come to her house and spend a few nights in her home. In return, she would receive bags of rice, pints of oil, chicken and beef, and other goods. On occasion, they would include some money with the merchandise.

"I was satisfied with the arrangement," explained the woman. "I didn't realize I was doing something wrong. I did not know that my guests were not married. Two years passed and the gifts and help improved my living condition. All of a sudden, my house was stormed by a group of officials. It seems that those storming my house had a disagreement with the officials who had made the arrangements with me. They stormed my house and accused me of running a prostitution ring. I was arrested. Now I realize that besides the prison sentence and exile, they want to confiscate my home. They claim that owning a property that has served as a center of corruption is against *sharia* law, and that the property must be turned over the coffers of the Islamic state."

Mama Pari and this old woman were both victims of poverty, and as a result they fell into the trap of corrupt officials within the Islamic Republic. These officials were the same people who boasted about Islamic values and morality and claimed to support the poor and disenfranchised. But they had acted in direct opposition to their own claims. One could say that the officials within the Islamic Republic shut down Shahre No so that they could establish similar efforts all over the country. Those behind these prostitution rings were the same people who would arrest and flog women for crimes of fraternization with men, poor *hejab* and enjoyment of music and dance.

I was still stunned from the discoveries I had made through these two cases when I went to a court that addressed crimes of immorality. We had entered the reform period and young Iranians had become more daring. Despite this, the reform period had not officially recognized women's right to use recreational facilities. Young girls 9 years old or older were still treated as adults and in cases where they had fraternized with men, had not observed the *hejab* appropriately or had been to parties with dance and music, they received punishments in line with their older counterparts. In this special morality court, I had the chance to witness yet another act of injustice that is regularly carried out against young women, in the name of Islam. I noted the occasion in my diary as follows:

The young girl could not be older than 17 years of age. Perhaps she is even younger than that. She has been sentenced to flogging. She seeks out her mother and in hurried manner approaches her. Her mother is a woman wearing the *chador* and is waiting for her in the public waiting area. The young girl asks for her mother's coat. She grabs the coat and wears it over her own. Her mother is crying.

The young girl turns to her mother and says: "Shhhh, how many times do I have to ask you not to cry? I know this place better than you. This is not my first time. I know what to do. Don't cry. It's not a big deal. A few strikes of the whip shouldn't warrant all this crying. My friends have experienced this before. They say that I should request immediately to receive my sentence. They wouldn't lie to me. They have taught me that I should wear two coats to protect against the pain of the whip. And I have heard that they don't strike that hard anyway. Now you just keep crying, as if the world has come to an end."

The mother continues her crying. In an effort to avoid the punishment, she begs her daughter to flee the courthouse. The girl leaves, bravely and without fear or embarrassment to ask for her punishment. The mother is both fearful and embarrassed and she hides her face behind her *chador*. I move toward the mother. Her crying takes on a high-pitched tone and she explains: "I am not crying because my daughter is going to suffer pain. I am crying because I know that from today everything will be normal for her. In a matter of one night, she will travel the route that should take years. No one can stop her now."

The young girl returns. She looks disoriented and defiant but still does not show any sense of fear. She explains that she is finished with her punishment. Her case is now closed. "Forget it!" she advises her mother, and then kisses her and hands back her coat. The mother and daughter hug and leave the courthouse.

I think to myself that it is quite possible that the person who carried out the sentence of the young girl, and flogged her, is also a customer of Mama Pari or the old woman who is now imprisoned for running a house of prostitution. I am amazed by all this contradiction and deceit – all in the name of Islam.

My disbelief and astonishment about what I was seeing in the cases and courts became unbearable when I received a phone call from my client "Mama Pari" from the city of Dubai in UAE, who had called to thank me for the unending troubles I went through for her to get her freedom. She said that she had opened a hairdressing salon in Dubai and was making a lot of money. I never understood how her sentence of 10 years of imprisonment was over turned without my notice, and she was able to leave the country and achieve such endless professional opportunities.

35

The year 1998 ended with parliamentary threats and four murders in the series of murders of intellectuals, commonly referred to as the "serial killings." Khatami had bravely announced that the murders had been committed by rouge elements within the Ministry of Information. The murderers were identified and the ministry cleansed of their presence. At the same time, these forces had been recruited by clandestine intelligence organizations connected with extremist conservatives. In the years that followed, especially 1999-2001, when the building of false cases exposing immorality of reformist figures reached a peak and was usually followed by their detention and physical and emotional torture, some of the leaders of the reform movement publicly announced that those responsible for the serial killings had not been eliminated from the system. Instead, they had just moved their operation to other locales. The reformist press was consumed with discussions on identifying those responsible for the serial killings.

When it was announced that the main suspect in the serial killings, Saied Islami, had committed suicide in prison, it was quickly rumored that those truly responsible for the serial killings had murdered Islami in an effort to keep from being exposed themselves. Experts believed that only Saied Islami had intricate knowledge of the serial murders and those responsible. Islami, it was believed, could incriminate officials at the highest levels within the Islamic Republic for these murders. In fact, a letter in this regard was published in the daily *Salam*, which resulted in its immediate closure.

A group of university students held peaceful demonstrations objecting to the closure of this daily. The demonstrations quickly turned violent at the hands of police and plain-clothes thugs associated with parallel clandestine intelligence groups under the control of extremist conservatives, who attacked the student dormitories, injured students and murdered one student.

After the start of the reform period, the student movement in Iran emerged as a peaceful movement in search of freedom. After the dormitory incident, the intelligence forces focused even more on the leaders of the student movement. Khatami's oppositional stance against the students seriously undermined his political credibility. By turning a peaceful demonstration violent, conservatives managed to bring Khatami closer to them, at least in the manner in which he dealt with and responded to the student protests and the student movement. After the crackdown against the student movement, it became clear that conservative forces were not going to back down and would continue with their violent tactics, without any regard for the millions of votes cast by Iranians in favor of reform. Despite this reality, the reformist press continued its criticism of the conservative establishment.

The political crisis that engulfed the nation as a result of the four serial murders, the crackdown against the student movement and the closure of the daily *Zan* (Woman) had marginalized discussions on women's rights. The discussions in the Fifth Parliament were focused on preventing and denying the right to criticize women's legal status within the press. These developments made it difficult for the two most vocal women's rights activists, Shirin Ebadi and myself, who had taken risks to discuss the issue of women's rights within the reformist press, to continue their activities unhindered. After the onset of political crises, it seemed that women's rights activists and writers focused more on the rights of the accused, especially those accused of press and political crimes, the serial murders, and the violence committed by those opposed to reform.

Few opportunities for criticizing the laws that discriminated against women presented themselves, and few dared present these issues for discussion passionately and steadfastly. I, too, focused on discussions related to other freedoms. Activist students, especially those active in the Office to Consolidate Unity (*Daftar-e Tahkim-e Vahdat*), did not allow the discussions on women's rights to die out. They continued these discussions by inviting well-known women's rights activists to speak at their forums and gatherings. What is of historical importance in this effort is the fact that male students would seek out the two most well-known advocates of women's rights—Shirin Ebadi and myself—more so than female students. These men would study our legal writings and interpretations about women's rights under the Islamic constitution with great care and would design precise questions, which were in fact an indication of their hopes and dreams.

I would become drunk with excitement at the site of both female students, wearing the *chador*, and male students who patiently awaited my arrival at the office. I felt that Iran was traveling an unparalleled historical route. On this route, young men and women knew exactly what they wanted. Feminism and the equality of rights was not only attractive for young female students, but for male students as well. Those female students who chose to observe strict Islamic dress because of their religious beliefs knew well that I was a secular thinker. They knew that my *hejab* was forced and they knew well that I had never supported the Islamic Revolution. Their presence in my law office— the office of a secular woman—and their efforts to popularize the discussions on women's rights demonstrated that religious revolutionaries were now beginning to examine the possibility of the separation of religion and state.

From their perspective, the violation of human rights in the name of safeguarding Islam was indefensible. Despite the fact that they personally respected interpretations of Islam and chose to observe the *hejab*, they criticized forced *hejab* and the laws that required it. In those days, student activists engaged in Islamic organizations included mostly students from traditional and religious families. These students, however, provided much needed support for those activists who dared to risk their own safety by defending human rights. They preferred to promote international human rights standards and human values instead of religious and Islamic doctrine. With this strategy, they worked to increase the value of their religion and their own legitimacy. When witness to the fact that some used violence in the name of Islam, they would become disheartened, but would work harder to find pathways out of the many dead ends that surrounded them. My law practice had turned into a place where religion and secular ideals could come to terms with one another, especially in the arena of women's rights.

I managed to make it through the crisis-filled year of 1998 while staying active. With the publication of *The Structure of Family Law in Iran, Women's Political Rights in Iran,* and *Eliminating Discrimination Against Women,* I had managed to increase the books I had authored. *Eliminating Discrimination Against Women* had been made possible through the cooperation of UNICEF and was published by Nashr-e Ghatreh. In this publication, Iranian law is compared to the Convention on the Elimination of all forms of Discrimination Against Women (CEDAW).

I felt that I lacked a certain something in my public life. Before May 23, 1997, and the start of the reform period in 1997, from the perspective of the government I was considered to be an outsider. As such, it had never occurred to me to set up a research organization. After the election of Mohammad Khatami, being under the impression that the divides between insider and outsider had disappeared, at least among the reformist sector of the government, I started the process of setting up an organization. With the help of my daughter Lily, who had studied law, and Zohreh Arzani, a young woman who was articling at the courts and who had worked with me for years, we set out to start an organization tasked with research on women's issues.

Ataollah Mohajerani was the minister of culture and Islamic guidance. In this position, he bravely and decisively worked against the Islamic extremists. I wrote the bylaws of the organization and submitted an application to one of offices of the Ministry of Culture and Islamic Guidance. Immediately following the submission of my application, I was asked to remove the name of my daughter Lily as a founding member. They explained that according to regulations, single women were not allowed to serve as founders of cultural centers. I removed her name from the application. The head of the office promised that he would treat my application favorably when it came up for review by the council charged with approving these types of applications. Several months passed, but I did not receive a reply, despite several attempts at inquiry. Finally I was informed that the council had declined my application to set up an organization. They had found me to be "unfit" for the task. Despite the fact that for years prior to the start of the official reform period in 1997 I had worked through reformist means to address the problems faced by society, in 1999 I was stopped cold at the borders of what defined me as an outsider, an other.

So it was such that my request to start the Center for Legal and Social Research on Women, submitted in July of 1999 to the secretariat in charge of cultural affairs at the Ministry of Culture and Islamic Guidance, was denied. With this denial, my opportunity to increase my own professional capacity withered as well. I never found out why I was found to be "unfit" to serve as a founder of a cultural and research center and why my application was denied. I never found out who the members of the council in charge of approving applications actually were.

My tumultuous life never afforded me the opportunity to examine or think about the hidden reasons and scenarios that worked to eliminate me from the political and cultural scenes and developments in Iran. Before being eliminated by the Ministry of Culture and Islamic Guidance under the direction of Ataollah Mohajerani, I had become a candidate for election for the board of directors of the Lawyers' Bar Association. The bar association was for the first time in the span of 20 years, in the year 1998 allowed to hold elections for the board. I was denied the opportunity to run for these elections as well. Then, too, I was found to be "unfit."

Both experiences held within them one message: In a theocracy, human rights and women's rights activists are distrusted and they should not be afforded the opportunity to organize. The energy and broad international relations that I had accumulated through my many years of experience could not be spent in service to my country. Instead it was spent trying to withstand the attack of invisible and visible swords so that I could maintain a presence within the Iranian political and cultural scenes. With every strike and attack, I would rise again. This battle with the Islamic Republic was indeed exhausting for my compatriots and me. On the other hand, I have no doubt that the theocracy, too, had tired and in many instances was forced to take a defensive stance and to retreat.

36

Young female university students quickly break the taboo of free association with the opposite sex, a fact that has their mothers distraught. The breaking of this taboo is much more noticeable within the context of the traditional fabric of life in the provinces. In my many trips to different areas of Iran during the second decade following the revolution, and with my witnessing the presence of women in public spaces, albeit religious women, I came to realize that the revolution at first glance succeeded in promoting a religious perspective among the Iranian population. But in reality, that religious perspective and belief has, as demonstrated through the overwhelming presence of women in the public sphere, worked in contradiction to its own message. Buses and minivans transport scores of young female university students, most of them sporting *chador*s, to the most remote locations of Iran, where the campuses of Azad University (Independent University) are based. Both young men and women from remote villages travel to the nearest university campuses where they have been accepted, in an effort to continue their education. And despite the fact that policies of segregation tend to dominate in the university environment—sometimes segregating the classes or separating the seating within classes—the reality remains that these policies, promoted by the Islamic government, have been unsuccessful in combating the true nature of men and women.

These young men and women don't waste any time in associating with one another, even in the few moments they spend on the bus en route to the university. In their backpacks, they carry cassette tapes of their favorite music, which is often Western or Iranian pop music deemed illegal. The minute they board the bus, they give the driver their cassette tapes and ask him to play their favorite songs. I witnessed such events on buses on several occasions.

Once, a group of young girls wearing *chador*s boarded a bus. One of them handed the driver a cassette tape and asked him to play it. He refused, claiming that it was a religious day of mourning. He explained that he was afraid of being stopped along the way. The illegal playing of music in a period of mourning would cause him trouble. The girls objected and gave him an ultimatum. If he did not play their music during the ride to the campus, they would vacate his bus and boycott him. As they disembarked, the boys on the bus followed, leaving only myself and few others on the bus. The driver continued his route between the two cities with only a few passengers. He explained that he was very worried. If these female students boycott his bus, he said, then the boys will follow them, and this would create financial problems for him. He explained that when the girls ride on his bus, the boys follow them. It is with a bus full of passengers that his route between cities will afford him enough profit to make his work worthwhile. Otherwise, the route is of no good and would not yield him enough of an income to offset his costs.

The driver was thinking out loud, and he decided that that night he would visit a young man in one of the villages who was in the business of copying bootleg music cassettes. The driver explained that he would only be able to attract these young customers if he were able to procure the most popular and up-to-date illegal music.

Iranian girls, in the second decade following the revolution, traveled across all cities and the roads and routes between them. Their movement was like the flight of crows that daily came closer to resembling the soaring of eagles.

Social changes were entirely visible and could have been seen from every angle, but the reformist government could not keep pace with the changes. The reformist movement was being slowed down constantly. Two obstacles prevented the movement of the government; one of them was an internal obstacle that was caused by the absence of a brave, powerful leader, a strong political party, and an organized, devised plan.

The external obstacle consisted of the legal limitations, the methods of oppression the conservatives were choosing to slow down the reform using all the legal and illegal tools at their disposal. All the while, people could see that the reform could not achieve their ideals, and slowly but surely were dispirited.

37

When Mohammad Khatami started his term as president and his reform government began work, the Fifth Parliament, with a conservative majority, had only served one year of its four-year term. The Fifth Parliament had a special role in the totality of the official policies designed to derail the reform process. From 1998, the members of this parliament, especially the female MPs, tried to implement several laws that were clear indications of their opposition to reform. The most significant of these proposals, which passed into law, defined the effort to defend and promote women's rights through the platform of the press as a crime to be met with a heavy punishment. Discussions about this proposal within the parliament demonstrated that a few women with ties to extremist conservative groups had taken the lead in drafting the bill. In their efforts to defend the bill, these women had pointed to a number of articles written by Shirin Ebadi and myself. These female parliamentarians had argued that it was indeed dangerous to allow Shirin Ebadi and me to continue our press-related activities, and that the continuation of our efforts would compromise Islam. Additionally, these female MPs had warned their colleagues in the parliament that should their bill not receive an appropriate number of votes necessary to pass into law, they would themselves take the lead in dealing with Shirin Ebadi and Mehrangiz Kar.[1]

In this political environment, the proposed bill was passed into law[2]. According to this bill, which became a law in 1377 (1998), the publication of articles that create conflict between

---

[1] For more about the role of female MPs, see the report in the addendum at the end of this book.

[2] Supplemental law, Paragraph B, Article 6 of the Press Law (1985), which bans the exploitation of images of women within publications.

men and women, or that support women's rights outside the context of *sharia*, are prohibited. Those violating this ban would be punished. The punishment, according to Article 698 of the penal code, includes a prison term of two months to two years or flogging (74 strikes). Additionally, should this crime be repeated more than once by a given publication, the press court has the right to shut down the publication.

A report in a newspaper, as reported by a parliamentary journalist, reads as follows: "The opinions expressed by some of the parliamentarians with respect to the passing of this bill were interesting. They created an environment within the parliament by which opposition to this bill was seen as opposition to the holy *sharia*.[3]"

The distinguishing factor between this bill and others put forth by extremist conservatives in the parliament was the focus placed on combating Shirin Ebadi and me. The threatening stance of the parliamentarians resulted in several international objections. The statement issued by international human rights organizations objects to the threats made against two female lawyers and reads as follows:

> His Excellency
> Hojjat ol-eslam Ali Akbar Nategh-Nouri
> Speaker of the Islamic Consultative Assembly
> Tehran, Iran
> May 19, 1998
>
> Your Excellency,
>
> The Lawyers Committee for Human Rights, Human Rights Watch, and the International Federation for Human Rights, three independent non-governmental organizations which work for the promotion and protection of human rights around the world, are writing to you to express their concern over comments made by a member of the Islamic Consultative Assembly (Majles) about prominent women lawyers in Iran. We fear that these comments may place the lawyers at risk of attack by vigilantes, and have

---

[3] "How was the bill banning the exploitation of women passed into law?"—Zahra Ibrahimi, *Hamshahri Daily*, Vol. 6, No. 1641, 6/23/1377 (Persian date, one year after the reform [1998]).

a chilling effect on the ability of lawyers to take part in public discussion of matters concerning the law, to the detriment of respect for the rule of law in the Islamic Republic of Iran.

During discussion in the Majles on April 12, 1998, about the amendment to Article 6 of the Press Law concerning the representation of women and the coverage of women's issues in the press, and making clear references to articles by prominent lawyers, it was threatened that "we are going to deal with these people ourselves." Although the women lawyers were not named in this instance, it was clear from references made that the women referred to were the lawyers Shirin Ebadi and Mehrangiz Kar.

While we recognize that opposing points of view should be expressed in the course of parliamentary debates, the words of parliamentarians should not legitimize political violence by zealots – such as the so-called Partisans of the Party of God, (Ansar-e Hezbollahi) - who take into their own hands the enforcement of religious orthodoxy. There is a pattern of statements by government officials or parliamentarians criticizing individuals or institutions being followed by vigilante violence. For example, on May 12, at a medical conference in Tehran, an Iranian surgeon who spoke out against a proposed law on gender segregation in health care was first strongly criticized by Dr. Dastjerdi, and one day later, beaten by Ansar-e Hezbollahi vigilantes at the same conference. The minister of the interior, Hojjat ol-eslam Abdollah Nouri, apologized to the surgeons, but no action has been taken to apprehend or prosecute these vigilantes.

The United Nations Basic Principles on the Role of Lawyers adopted by the Eighth U.N. Congress on the Prevention of Crime and the Treatment of Offenders and welcomed by the 45th General Assembly of the U.N., with the assent of the Islamic Republic, on December 14, 1990, sets out guarantees necessary for the functioning of lawyers. They provide in Principle 16 that:

Governments shall ensure that lawyers are able to perform all of their professional functions without intimidation, hindrance, harassment or improper interference; ...

In relation to lawyers' right to freedom of expression and association the Basic Principles provide in Principle 23:

… In particular, they [lawyers] shall have the right to take part in public discussion of maters concerning the law …

In their comments on laws affecting women, Ms. Ebadi and Ms. Kar were exercising their internationally recognized right to comment on matters concerning the law and to promote the cause of justice and human rights. The nature and tone of comments made by the members of the Majles mentioned above could have led to harmful consequences to the personal security of the individuals concerned and detrimental to the process of considered law making in the Islamic Republic.

As speaker of the Majles, we respectfully urge you to promote and welcome the involvement of lawyers in public debate of matters concerning the law in the Islamic Republic as being in the best interests of the society. We ask that you condemn irresponsible comments from members of the Majles that may endanger the personal security of lawyers exercising their fundamental rights.

Thank you for your consideration of these matters.

Sincerely,

Neil Hicks
Senior Program Coordinator
Lawyers Committee for Human Rights

Hanny Megally
Executive Director
Middle East Division
Human Rights Watch

Patrick Baudoin
President
Federation of Internationale des Ligues de Droits de l'Homme

I didn't leave the threats of the members of the Fifth Parliament unanswered. I knew that a direct response to Dr. Vahid-

Dastjerdi, who represented an extremist conservative point of view, would be dangerous. I did not pay attention to these dangers. By using the conducive environment provided by the reformist press, I wrote an article in response to her threats. The article, titled "Women against Women," responded directly and frankly to those who were opposed to freedom of speech. The text of the article reads as follows:

"Women Against Women:Exploitation of Women in the Political Realm."

Adineh Monthly, No. 127, June 1998, Pages 12-13

The proposal to add an amendment to the 6th article of the 4th section of the Press Law was approved by the Islamic Parliament on the 23rd of Farvardin (April 1998). Should this proposed law be implemented, the discussions with respect to women's rights within the press will become either extremely difficult or impossible. The amendment reads as follows: "Exploitation of women, either in the form of images or in the form of content, insulting of women, encouragement of luxuries, promotion of conflict between men and women through defense of women's rights outside of the law and *sharia*" by the press is in violation of the Press Law. A few women within the parliament have worked extensively, using their powers and connections, to secure approval of this law. In so doing, they have used threats, organized women against women for their own political agendas, and have used the legislative body as a venue to promote and implement a particular line of thinking. Reports from the discussions of the Fifth Parliament in this respect demonstrate that Ms. Vahid-Dastjerdi has threatened other members of parliament into voting for this legislation and has explicitly stated that if the members of parliament don't approve her proposed measure she will enter into action on her own. Below is a statement she made in the Majles:

"... If there are people who in the name of defending women's rights are willing to oppose concepts such as *dieh*, other main pillars of beliefs within Islam, martyrdom, inheritance laws, and other doctrine within the holy Koran, we will deal with these people ourselves. If the honorable members of the parliament are unwilling to vote for this amendment, they should know that we will carry out our religious duty, and deal with these people ourselves. But, let me point out that it is not appropriate that an amendment meant to protect women's rights, designed to protect women's status and honor, meant to strengthen women's independence, and seeking to improve their value within society, is not approved by the Islamic Parliament, in an Islamic system."

Do these threats, uttered by a female member of parliament, not call for addressing political and legal experts with the following questions: Do members of parliament, charged with legislative duties, have the right to use threats to gain support for their proposals? Do members of parliament have the right to weaken the law, by making statements that call for taking the law into their own hands, in the absence of support for their proposals? Doesn't this strategy of defense in fact question the credibility of the lawmaker? I would like to know exactly against whom Ms. Vahid-Dastjerdi intends to take action. Why is it that she, under the pretense of defending women's rights, has tried to deny women the right to defend their rights through the press? Why is she building cases against people who have tried to explain and clarify the discriminatory laws against women, accusing them of the high crime of acting against the Koran? Why, in the name of carrying out her legislative duties, does she want to sanction the murder of these individuals? Is this kind of defense in the best interest of a system which is bound by laws, and which seeks to work within the framework of the constitution that calls on each of the three branches of government to have certain defined and limited rights and ability for action? Hasn't this honorable MP stepped far beyond her own set of responsibilities and duties? Does she, a member of parliament, charged with setting laws, have the right to speak in this manner? Based on what doctrine does she suppose that she has the unlimited power to take action against these people herself even without the approval of the legal measure she is putting forth? Who exactly does she intend to take action against? The people she is referring to are two women writers, whose writings she had selected and read in support of her proposal during the hearing on this issue within parliament. Why did the honorable chair of the meeting not issue a warning against this type of speech? Why was Ms. Vahid-Dastjerdi not warned that the sentence, "... we will deal with these people ourselves," is a statement of revenge and that the parliament is no place for airing statements of this kind? Why did no one ask this MP why she was using the platform afforded her through the parliament for setting limits and threatening individuals? Why did no other member of parliament point out that the parliament, where laws are adopted, is not a suitable place for the breaking of the law?

Presuming that this MP has extended her powers beyond the limits defined by the law in announcing that she herself will take action against those who defy her, I ask of her: Who exactly are you seeking to take action against and how? Perhaps it is with me and the other woman who has dared to write about the discriminatory laws against women. Perhaps you are seeking to take action against clerics, researchers, and alternative religious thinkers and intellectuals who have rightfully learned and believe that it is Islam which suffers at the hands of people like yourself, who without examination or analysis support discriminatory laws and force them upon society as absolutes and uncontested religious doctrine. Are you taking action against those who have been waiting for years in the hopes that you, and those whose thinking is in line with yours, will take a moment to review the laws of this land and spend time in the family courts, so that you may be informed about the lack of legal support provided by the system for the women of this country?

Who have you tried to frighten with this statement? Are you trying to frighten the people who have for years risked their lives, compromised their positions, their resources, and other benefits, and who have endured endless insult? Who are you trying to frighten? The same people who have in the most difficult of circumstances chosen to write in an effort to protect their own rights, without fear of the consequences of their actions? The strategy of inflicting fear that you have chosen is indicative of the fact that you yourself are frightened. It seems that you are frightened that with future legislative bodies you will be unable to insist on this issue. It seems that you are frightened of your own inability to effectively respond to the reasonable inquiries and demands of women with respect to their rights and that you will lose your opportunity to be elected to the parliament for another term. Simply put, you will not have a satisfying response to the questions of women who wonder what it is that you have done for them as a member of parliament. The sense of fear can be felt in your words and your manner of speech. It is apparent that in your efforts to take on an offensive stance, you are in actuality trying to mask your defensive and powerless mode. You are afraid that perhaps history will not judge you kindly, as you have made Islam your excuse to break the pen of the few writers who don't fear anyone but God. You believe that if you can marginalize these few women, other young and energetic women who have taken up the task of writing in the press, and who soon will be threatening your power by asking similar questions about women's rights, will be silenced and will let you be, so that you can continue to rest on your legislative powers and, with the excuse of protecting human dignity, make it illegal for anyone to question the law, which I suppose in your opinion is in line with Islamic doctrine.

You have achieved a position that allows you to threaten the parliament into realizing your goals. Keep in mind that you owe your position to the women who joined the revolution in the belief that their legal rights would be advanced. It is ludicrous to assume that a nation would join a revolution with the goal of decreasing their legal rights. Women's entrance into the political realm has been made possible by the demands of the people for justice, especially the demands of Iranian women. But your interpretation of Islam is not the only interpretation, nor is it necessarily the correct one. You should know that Islamic doctrine does not give you the right to assume that what you want is right and what other informed women advocate for with respect to the negative impact of laws on their lives is wrong.

Iranian women are not forced to succumb to their own lower social status. For example, they are not forced to accept that the price of the *dieh* (blood money) is half that of men. They are not forced to accept that if their female relative is murdered they have to pay the difference in blood money to the family of the murderer in order to see justice done. Iranian women do not have to accept that their inheritance is less than their brothers', nor do they

have to accept that men should forever have absolute
rights to divorce. They do not have to accept that the
custody of their children after divorce is solely with their
husbands, nor do they have to accept the fact that 9-year-
old girls are treated under our legal system as adults and
subject to adult punishments under the penal code.
Women don't have to accept that the fathers of young
girls or their paternal grandfathers have the right to wed
their daughters and granddaughters without their consent
(from their birth onwards). Iranian women do not have to
allow or accept that their husbands and fathers-in-law
would face no punishment should they murder their children. Iranian women do not have to accept the practice of
being barred from judicial benches and other similar positions.

This honorable member of parliament through the use of
threats has created an impression in the minds of the people that perhaps certain political groups are misusing
women as their strategy. Defending a bill should not require threats or the creation of false cases against individuals. She could have simply defended the proposed bill
based on logic that argued the effort as essential.

Given that the proposed legislation is only a repetition of
existing law, and has even failed to observe the criteria
essential to drafting good legislation, it seems that this
proposal is really intended to promote personal beliefs
and to take revenge on a few writers who have addressed
women's rights through the press. It seems that this proposal is actually intended to put out accusations against
persons whose writing is based on the law and legal doctrine—an act which does not need to be addressed
through another law. I should warn that we as writers are
not to be underestimated. Those who have become active
in the area of analyzing and criticizing the law can be likened to Galileo. It is true that they don't enjoy much support. It is true that they may easily be banned from the
press scene, or even denied their life, but whenever afforded the opportunity and under all circumstances they
will claim that "the earth is round!" Eliminating them
from the scene will not make the earth square. Let me say
it frankly: The laws of Iran will not and cannot respond to
the needs and demands of today's society and in fact have
rendered women quite powerless in protecting their own

human dignity. Ms. Vahid-Dastjerdi, let me warn you and your co-workers who have worked so hard to pass this bill into law that we have to review our existing laws. This is a reality that will happen— sooner or later and regardless of whether you are successful in passing your bill into law, it will happen. You cannot use the excuse of defending human dignity to oppose the human rights and demands of half the population. You cannot stop Iranian women, who have started on the path of realizing their rights, from continuing on this path. Nor can you stop those who are lighting this path with their ideas. Nor can you change the direction of this path. Opposing this movement is not logical, nor is it beneficial. The best interest of the Islamic Republic, to which you are dedicated, dictates that you stop this opposition.

Epilogue

I should explain that from the time this article was published, my confrontation with those who could aptly be named as setting the foundational thinking of the regime became overt. After this direct confrontation with extremist Islamic conservatives, the events in my personal and social life took on a new form. I hope to discuss these events in future memoirs. This memoir—a journey that started with the need for persistence and caution, needs which were eased by the journey's end—will now come to a close.

Men have written history. The history of Iran has consistently been told from a male perspective. The practice of writing memoirs, which is indeed the best form for the telling of history, has been exclusively a male domain. But the current history of Iran cannot be written by men alone. The current history, which has taken shape around femininity, can only be understood through a micro-perspective. Despite its male appearance, the history of Iran after the Islamic Revolution has taken on a truly feminine essence. The major historical developments in Iran's recent history have emerged around a feminine core. The Islamic regime of Iran initiated its violence with the excuse of defending and protecting the honor of women. It has even been able to effectively mobilize women against women in this endeavor. The strategy of appropriating the personal identities of its citizens, in particular women, including even the color of their dress, has been a central policy of the Islamic regime. The religious and secular identities of Iranian women have taken shape under the attacks of the Islamic Republic. These two identities have created a major challenge for all the values that the regime promotes.

I am only one of the players in Iran's new history. My good fortune has afforded me some notoriety. But Iranian women, without enjoying fame or notoriety, have forced their individual and female identities upon this eventful history. They have lived and died anonymously, and despite the fact that they joined the forces of the revolution in the masses in 1979, they have managed with the passing of time to discover their personal identities.

On a spring morning of the year 2000, I woke up in solitary confinement in the Evin prison. That day I remembered that in the contemporary history of Iran, in the last 100 years, whenever this nation has awakened and started a spring, that spring has suffered an autumn.

My crime was that, at the international Berlin Conference that took place in April of 2000 under the title of "Iran after the reform," I had said that reform couldn't be instated using the current constitution of Iran. That following year, my husband, Siamak Pourzand, was arrested and spent a few of his olden years in the jail and under torture. He is now under house arrest in Iran and cannot leave the country. I left Iran before my husband's arrest and with the help of the European Union, to seek medical treatment for my cancer, and cannot return to Iran. My numerous requests for return to my homeland under secure conditions are unofficially declined. In these conditions, Lily and Azadeh have suffered many psychological, financial and emotional damages. They have lost their home, natural family life and happiness in Iran. They miss their father and they are sad to not be able to take care of him. Reform has failed and those who opposed reform are currently in power in Iran. Iran is standing on the edge of war and other new problems. Millions of Iranians inside and outside of Iran are praying, hoping for a miracle. A miracle is their only hope of ever achieving freedom.

Mehrangiz Kar
Spring 2006

Addendum

When the term of the Fifth Parliament had come to a close, a number of women's organizations held a meeting to evaluate the performance of female MPs of the Fifth Parliament. Shirin Ebadi and I were present at this meeting. Women MPs associated with extremist conservative groups declined the invitation, but Faezeh Hashemi, Soheila Jelodarzadeh and Fatemeh Ramezanzadeh, who represented a moderate point of view, did attend. The meeting provided Shirin Ebadi and me an opportunity to evaluate and criticize the policies and the performance of the female MPs. A report of this meeting has been provided on the Internet site "Bad Jens" (www.badjens.com), which is managed by Mahsa Shekarloo, as follows:

Female Members of the 5th Majles Confront the Public

On Feb.7, 2000, all fourteen female members of the 5th Majles (chamber of parliament) were invited to a public question-and-answer forum to account for their performances as policymakers regarding women's issues in Iran. The event was organized by the groundbreaking and highly esteemed feminist-Islamist women's magazine *Zanan* (Women), and by Roshangaran Press—headed by Ms. Laheji, a long-time publisher and women's rights advocate. All fourteen members had accepted the invitation, but only three, Faezeh Hashemi, Sohelia Jelodarzadeh, and Fatemeh Ramzanzadeh (arriving an hour late), actually came.

Most of the 100 people in attendance in the amphitheatre of the Enghelab Physical Fitness Club (prior to the revolution, the private and exclusive Shah-an-shahi Club), located in one of the affluent areas in the north of Tehran, were "secular" activist women. Only a handful were men, with half of these being Iranian and foreign reporters, including one French journalist, shuffling through the rows of seats with his cameraman and his Iranian (female) guide, looking for women in the audience who could *parle francais*. Save for a few glances at the now familiar sight of a foreign journalist eager for the latest scoop on women in Iran, most of the audience looked on indifferently.

The event began with everyone standing up for the Iranian national anthem, the recitation of a prayer, a reading of a poem (played to soft background music, until someone yelled, "Put it off"), followed by salutations, thanks, and introductions. The moderator of the discussion, Fereshteh Ta'erpour, declared that the goal of the forum was to critically analyze the representatives' legislative activities within the last four years in the Majles, so that more enlightened paths for progress, a better political understanding, and better results could be reached. She added, "The candidates for the 6th Majles should keep in mind that they, too, will be faced with a day such as this, where they will have to answer for their actions."

The composition of the 6th Majles is considered to be a determining factor in the political future of Iran. The whole nation, especially reformists, is concerned about the tense competition for power now exploding into a backlash of violence between various social and political groups. This unprecedented face-to-face meeting between grassroots women activists and members of the Majles was a mutual acknowledgement of the growing emphasis and necessity for dialogue.

Moreover, the MPs represented a particular segment of Islamic society of which many in the audience did not consider themselves part. And yet, many of them were elected by precisely this group of onlookers, who simply felt it important to have female members in the Majles. Faezeh Hashemi, who during the 5th Majles elections was the top vote getter in Tehran— before being bumped down to number two to make room for conservative cleric Nategh-Nouri—was now being faced with an edgy, impatient crowd of constituents, demanding to know what she'd done for them, and how she had improved their lives.

Hashemi, whose daily newspaper *Zan* (Woman) was unconstitutionally shut down one year ago, spoke of the two factors that she believed had led to the lack of unity between the female members of the Majles. Dressed in a red sweater, black and white checkered headscarf, blue jeans, black boots, and a *chador*, she said, "During the first year and a half, factional issues and other conflicts [...] were non-existent between women. Despite our differing viewpoints, when it came to women's issues, we were unified, coordinated, and of the same mind. As a result, we were able to pass 22 items of legislation concerning women. However, two significant events caused the erasure of this unity: The first splitting between women occurred when two particular items of legislation came up, both of which stood in opposition to the executive branch of the government: prohibiting the "exploitation" (*estefade-ye abzari*) of women's images in publications, and mandating sexual segregation within the medical field to comply with religious canon. The second splitting occurred during the banning of the newspaper, Zan, after which women's issues were given less attention."

With the exception of Hashemi and Fatemeh Ramzanzadeh, every female member signed the above widely contested legislation. And, Hashemi added, "Before the 5th Majles, I used to think that the presence of any woman in the Majles, regardless of leaning or viewpoint, is to the benefit of women. But now, I believe that their perspective and outlook are extremely important, and we must be aware of this."

Ms. Jelodarzadeh spoke of the members' accomplishments, stressing that although they did not successfully tackle many of the issues important to women, they did make a substantial effort. Both Jelordarzadeh and Hashemi pointed fingers at the media for not reporting on their attempts to bring women's issues to national attention. Female members of the Majles are barred from being shown on television, which is under the grip of the conservative faction within the government. Ms. Hashemi insisted that much as she spoke about women, it was never reported by the media, and that the only statements that were ever published were about issues unrelated to women.

Following their short speeches, attorneys Mehrangiz Kar and Shirin Ebadi, two of the most prominent women's rights activists in Iran, directed their statements to the MPs. Kar began by noting the repetitious nature of her own discourse, complaining that she had been saying the same things over and over again for several years. She acknowledged the members' difficulties while reminding them of the opportunities available to them, "We, too, know that in a Majles which addressed women like commodities, and spoke of their 'depreciating value', the female representatives have had difficulties, yet this does not mean that there was no platform available to you." She asked why the legal age of puberty for a girl was still nine years, and why she could still be punished as an adult, and why women still had limited divorce rights. She stated that Iranian society itself hadn't accepted such laws, and that Iranian women weren't done with, but were alive and vibrant. Islam, she added, could indeed solve these issues for the people, but so far it had not. "How is Islam to do this," she asked.

Shirin Ebadi, for her part, spoke of being tired of repeating herself, and stressed the precedence of civil rights over political ones. She rhetorically asked, "Is it really an honor to have a female vice-president who, when she wants to leave the country, must bow her head to her husband and ask him for permission?" She wanted to know why, when women speak of their rights, they were accused of questioning the precepts of Islam. She claimed that it was women's religious duty to challenge the Majles' denial of women's rights, and deeply regretted that the majority of women members voted for legislation against women.

Ms. Jelordazadeh, apparently hoping that a double standard might at least alleviate Ebadi's discontent, reassured everyone that female officials in the government didn't need their husbands' permission for exiting the country. (So if certain things aren't quite so rigid, perhaps this simply means that women in the government are leaving the rest of their sisters behind.)

After the rebuttals, the remaining time was left for the candidates for the 6th Majles to present themselves. By the time they had each delivered a short speech about their intentions and beliefs, the time was up, and the audience was unable to directly question the members. As much as they were disappointed, most women believed that the event, on the whole, was a successful step in the right direction. At best, the sense of difference and separation became a bit smaller that day- the gap between "us" and "them" narrowed as the women on the podium shared their hardships. The representatives became less of an inaccessible group.

Faezeh Hashemi herself admitted that if this meeting had taken place earlier, maybe they would have approached things differently in the Majles: "Maybe we would have taken you into account more." The audience broke into loud applause in approval. In her case, the acknowledgement came too late, and she suffered the consequences during these last elections. Women, angered by what some perceive as her buckling to conservative pressure, and her unquestioning support of her powerful father, withdrew their support, which resulted in her failed attempt at re-election (her father is the unpopular Hashemi Rafsanjani, who was president of the Islamic Republic for two terms).

The forum was an attempt, in the face of the absence of institutionalized democratic processes, to apply pressure to elected public officials. In a nation where there are very few independent public forums available, especially to women, and there are no formal political avenues through which people can communicate, there is a lack of information about, and amongst women. There are hardly any statistics speaking to their condition, much less their viewpoints, and there are few systems in place for women to directly communicate with each other. It's almost as if the only things they have and know are their immediate surroundings. Perspectives, ideas, and information remain fragmented. With the events of this day, the limited scope possibly widened a little on both sides. As if by coincidence, the next day, Jelodarzadeh was quoted in a newspaper addressing women's issues.

The event provided a chance for dialogue between what one might call "religious" and "secular" women, who were able to share the overall difficulties of womanhood. Yet part of what the said secular women tried to communicate was that, although some women in society had advanced by entering the public realm, there were others who had suffered. A "look at me too, while you've moved forward, I've been left behind. Be aware that it's been at my expense." Differing realities were presented that day.